Luv Questions

650 questions, quotes and fun facts about everyone's favorite subject

Cyndi Haynes

SOURCEBOOKS CASABLANCA™
AN IMPRINT OF SOURCEBOOKS, INC.®
NAPERVILLE, ILLINOIS

Published by Sourcebooks, Inc.
P.O. Box 4410, Naperville, Illinois 60567-4410
(630) 961-3900
FAX: (630) 961-2168
www.sourcebooks.com

Library of Congress Cataloging-in-Publication Data

Haynes, Cyndi.
   Luv questions : 650 question, quotes and fun facts about
everyone's favorite subject / by Cyndi Haynes.
      p. cm.
   ISBN 1-40220-127-3 (alk. paper)
 1. Mate selection. 2. Love. 3. Dating (Social customs) 4. Man-
woman relationships. I. Title: Love questions. II. Title.
HQ801 .H378 2003
306.82—dc21

                                                    2003009786

          Printed and bound in the United States of America

              VP 10 9 8 7 6 5 4 3 2

Dedication

This book is dedicated in loving memory to Margaret Oswald Sparrenberger, who helped to plant so many wonderful seeds in me and to Carol Andreae Haynes, who always took an enormous interest in my life. I miss you both so very much. I love you and thank you from the bottom of my heart for all you've done for me.

Acknowledgments

Todd Stocke, thank you for believing in me and introducing me to Deborah Werksman.

Deborah Werksman, I hope you know how very much I appreciate all of your hard work on this book. Laura Kuhn, thank you for being a great copy editor.

Finally, to all of the individuals at Sourcebooks who worked on this project, I am very grateful for your help.

Other books by Cyndi Haynes

Keeping Love Alive

The Book of Friendship

The Book of Change

2002 Ways to Cheer Yourself Up

*2002 Ways to Show Your Kids
You Love Them*

Other books by Cyndi Haynes
and Dale Edwards

2002 Questions and Answers for Lovers

2002 Romantic Ideas

*2002 Ways to Find, Attract, and
Keep a Mate*

2002 Ways to Say, "I Love You"

2002 Things to Do on a Date

Dear Reader,

I believe that Plato was right when he wrote, "The unexamined life is not worth living." I hope these questions and tidbits validate some of your thoughts, jar your thinking a bit, and most of all, I hope you have an epiphany somewhere among these pages that changes your love life!

Whether you read this book by yourself in the privacy of your own home, or take it with you to read over lunch with your girlfriends, it will help you find your best path in the complicated world of dating. Sydney J. Harris stated, "Ninety percent of the world's woe comes from people not knowing themselves, their abilities, their faults, and even their real virtues. Most of us go almost all the way through life as complete strangers to ourselves." I promise you that if you answer the questions in this book, you will most assuredly know yourself, your love life, dreams, and how you want to find your own unique road to your happily-ever-after ending.

Happy questioning,

Cyndi Haynes

Put your ear down close
to your soul and listen hard.

Anne Sexton

1

Did you know that most people marry someone who lives within an eight-mile radius of their home?

♥ If you are looking for love, this should inspire you to get out among your neighbors.

♥ If, however, you don't like your neighbors, it may be the right time to consider moving to a neighborhood that has more singles with your lifestyle preferences.

2

Do you ever think about how Mr. Right might be in your life right now and you just haven't started dating him yet?

❤ Write out a list of all of the single men you know. Ask yourself if there are any men that you might want to consider dating. If the answer is yes, start making some plans.

> On the human chessboard,
> all moves are possible.
>
> William Blake

Do you ever think that the date you are trying so hard to impress tonight might turn out to be someone you gladly dump three weeks from now?

Why not worry about the impression your date is making on you instead of feeling insecure about your own impression?

Did you know that 93 percent of the U.S. population get married?

❤ That should calm your fears about never finding Mr. Right.

❤ The odds are stacked in your favor.

Tell me thine company, and I'll tell thee what thou art.

Miguel de Cervantes

Do you ever think about the psychological theory that says we attract to us those who are most like us?

♥ Ask yourself if you would want to date someone like yourself. If not, maybe you should consider doing a little self-improvement work.

Do you ever think about the fact that you can have only one first kiss and one first love?

♥ Why spoil them with Mr. Wrong?

What does your romantic track record say about you?

♥ Spend an hour writing your dating history. Look for any patterns. Learn from your mistakes and celebrate your triumphs.

8

Do you ever think that the person sitting across from you on your date tonight could be the love of your life?

Just thinking about it should help to put a little smile on your face.

When one door closes another door opens; but we so often look so long upon the closed door that we do not see the ones which open for us.

Alexander Graham Bell

Did you know that most singles wish that they were married and most married people wish they were single?

♥ It is key to marry only when you are ready to settle down and only when you truly find Mr. Right.

We all long for love; everything else is just killing time.

Kenny Loggins

10

Do you ever think about your date's budget if he is picking up the tab?

♥ The average cost of a first date is $29.50.

11

Do you ever think about joining a dating service?

♥ Business at dating services jumped 17 percent the first few months after 9/11 and continues to flourish.

Do you ever think about the sobering statistics that 50 percent of all first marriages end in divorce, 60 percent of all second marriages end in divorce, and a whopping 70 percent of all third marriages end in divorce?

♥ You have got to do your homework. You must be happy with yourself, pick the right person, and do it all at the right time to put the odds in your favor.

Do you usually buy
something new to wear
on a first date (even though
your date hasn't seen your
dating wardrobe before)?

You aren't alone. Seventy-eight percent of
women report buying something new to wear
before an important first date.

> Many persons of high
> intelligence have notoriously
> poor judgment.
>
> Sydney J. Harris

14

What is your biggest love-life fear?

💜 Most singles, both men and women, report that their three biggest fears regarding their love lives are rejection, fear of failure, and fear of success.

15

Are your daily activities and your routine helping or hurting your love life?

💜 You can't be a shy couch potato and have an exciting love life.

16

Do you ever think about your old flame?

♥ Why? Do you really want him back, or are you just wasting your time?

17

Do you follow your heart or your head concerning love-life issues?

♥ Studies suggest that the happiest women use both their heads and their hearts when picking a mate.

18

How many times have you continued to date someone you knew was wrong for you?

♥ Stop that! You are just wasting your time and your peace of mind.

> Analyze your life in terms of its environment. Are the things around you helping you toward success—or are they holding you back?
>
> W. Clement Stone

19

Do you ever think about taking a self-defense class?

♥ Fifty percent of all sexual assaults occur on dates.

♥ Thirty percent of all female homicide victims are killed by their husbands, ex-husbands, or boyfriends.

♥ Eighty percent of all victims of sexual assaults know their attackers.

We each need to let our intuition guide and then be willing to follow the guidance directly and fearlessly.

Shakti Gawain

20

What are your thoughts right before a big date?

♥ Are you positive or negative?

21

Do you ever think about dating a younger man?

♥ The LA Times reports that in 1995, 23.5 percent of women married younger men, and for women ages 33 to 44, that figure increased to 41 percent.

Do you ever dwell on the mistakes you know you have made with regard to your love life?

Just remember that mistakes can be great learning tools and can help you a great deal if you learn from them. The key to success is to learn the lesson quickly and then move on.

> Insanity is doing the same thing again and again but expecting different results.
>
> UNKNOWN

23

Do you believe that you have to kiss a lot of toads before you find your prince?

♥ The average American woman dates twenty-nine men before meeting Mr. Right.

> Flops are a part of life's menu, and I've never been a girl to miss out on any of the courses.
>
> Rosalind Russell

24

What are you willing to sacrifice for your true love?

♥ King Edward gave up the British throne in 1936 to marry the love of his life, Wallis Simpson.

25

Do you ever think about how you would pay for your dream wedding?

♥ The average wedding in the United States now costs more than nineteen thousand dollars.

Do you ever think about how many weddings you will attend in your lifetime and how these special occasions are a great place to meet eligible men?

The average person is invited to 2.2 weddings a year.

Know thine opportunity.
Pihacus

Do you ever think about trying to meet Mr. Right online?

❤ It is the fastest-growing way for people to meet.

❤ Twenty-two million singles have dated online.

> A woman has got to love a bad man once or twice in her life to be thankful for a good one.
>
> Mae West

28

Do you ever think about asking for God's help with your love life?

♥ God has a plan for your life and wants you to be happy and fulfilled.

♥ Singles who have a rich spiritual life report being happier.

> Ye have not,
> because ye ask not.
>
> James 4:2

Do you ever think about dating someone of a different race?

♥ Interracial dating has been steadily on the rise in the past decade.

It doesn't hurt to be optimistic. You can always cry later.

Lucimar Santos de Lima

30

Do you ever wonder if you are too old to find true love?

♥ Gloria Steinem married for the first time at age sixty.

♥ Elizabeth Barrett, the famous poetess, married Robert Browning when she was thirty-nine and had their baby at forty-three.

♥ The moral of the story is to never give up your search for love.

Keep breathing.

Sophie Tucker

31

Do you ever think about how your guardian angel is watching your dating behavior?

♥ Do you find that thought comforting?

32

Do you ever think about how the clock is ticking?

♥ Make sure that you enjoy your life, whether you have a mate in it or not.

Do you ever think about the time when your love life was at its best?

💙 What can you learn from that time?

💙 Can you do anything to recreate that level of happiness?

> Life is short; live it up.
> Nikita Khrushchev

Do you ever think about how you and your girlfriends could change each other's love lives for the better?

♥ Brainstorm with each other. Be creative about your approach to dating.

Sometimes small things lead to great joys.

S. Y. Agnon

Do you ever think about what gifts from old boyfriends are most precious to you and why?

Make your gifts to your current love reflect three things. Number one: make the gift reflect his interests. Number two: make the gift unique by having it personalized in some way. Finally: always present a gift to a beau in a wonderfully wrapped presentation to make it even more memorable.

36

Do you ever think that what you say or do today may drastically change another person's life?

♥ Keep in mind that you might be the answer to someone else's prayers.

♥ Remember to help your girlfriends with their love life-problems. Who knows, you may be the world's best matchmaker!

♥ Understand that your demeanor may cause someone to ask you out or not to ask you out.

♥ Pay close attention to your actions. Mr. Right may be watching!

Do you ever think about how most people will fantasize about their first love for the rest of their lives?

💜 Savor each special moment that comes along.

💜 Start a great scrapbook to hold precious mementos and photos.

> Never frown, because you never know who might be falling in love with your smile.
>
> Justine Milton

38

Do you ever think that if you devote an hour a day to improving your love life that at the end of the year you will have completed 365 hours of self-improvement?

♥ Read self-help books on dating.

♥ Join a new club, start a new hobby.

♥ Develop new friendships with men and women.

♥ Exercise. You will look and feel better. Furthermore, you might meet Mr. Right at the gym.

39

Do you ever think how this year may turn out to be the very best year of your love life?

♥ Have faith.

♥ Don't get discouraged.

40

Do you ever think about how looks fade and youth can't be recaptured?

♥ Never marry a man for what is on the outside.

Do you ever think about what your love life would be like if you had lived a hundred years ago or a thousand years ago?

♥ Knowing that on a dateless Saturday night you can sit in your air-conditioned home, reading a magazine, while watching the latest DVD, waiting for your pizza to be delivered doesn't seem so bad when you compare it to what life would have been like in the past.

♥ Plus, most women don't have a thing for the caveman type!

42

Do you ever think that
the knowledge that is
most important in your
love life probably wasn't
learned in school?

♥ Where did you get your dating philosophy?

♥ Who was your role model?

♥ Does your view of male/female relationships
need a tune-up?

43

Do you ever think about how your date has similar fears, dreams, hopes, and desires?

♥ Relax, we are all human.

44

Do you ever think about past roads not taken?

♥ Is it too late to take them now?

45

Do you ever think about how your life would be if you had been born as a member of the opposite sex?

Do you think it would be easier or harder? Why? Try to see the world from the other sex's point of view.

Oh, I'm scared all the time. I just act as if I am not.

Katharine Hepburn

When you are angry at a date, do you ever think what it would be like if you had been born with his genes, had his life experiences, and held his belief system?

Compassion and empathy are two of the most important qualities found in happy marriages.

Any fool can criticize, condemn, and complain— and most fools do.

Dale Carnegie

47

Do you ever think that some of your most treasured memories will be of holidays, vacations, and other times spent with family?

♥ Never neglect beloved family members to pursue your love life. Find a happy balance.

48

How quickly do you fall in love?

♥ Most married men say that they fell in love with their wives by the fifth date.

49

Does it sometimes seem as if everyone is married but you?

♥ There are fewer than fifty-five million married couples in the U.S.

♥ The good news is that there are millions more singles than marrieds.

50

Are you an optimist or a pessimist when it comes to love?

♥ Studies prove that optimists are happier in love and life. Lighten up!

51

Do you ever think about how it takes more facial muscles and more energy to frown than it does to smile?

♥ Put on a happy face. You will look better and studies prove that even if you fake a smile, it will make you feel better.

What can be gained by sailing to the moon if we are not able to cross the abyss that separates us from ourselves? This is the most important of all voyages of discovery and without it all the rest are not only useless, but disastrous.

Thomas Merton

5²

Do you ever think about why women wear their engagement rings and their wedding bands on the third finger of their left hand?

♥ The answer dates back to ancient times when people believed that the third finger on the left hand was the only finger having a vein that connected to the heart.

A diamond is a chunk of coal made good under pressure.

UNKNOWN

42

Do you ever think about what your engagement ring will look like?

❤ The average ring is .75 carat weight.

❤ One third of all engagement and wedding bands are platinum.

❤ Seventy-six percent of all engagement rings are solitaires.

❤ More than 90 percent of all engagement rings are diamonds.

❤ Seventy-five percent of engaged women receive an engagement ring.

54

How long would you like your engagement period to last?

♥ The traditional engagement period lasts one year.

55

What questions would you like to ask your guardian angel, your mentor, or your heroine regarding your love life?

♥ Can you find the answers to those questions within yourself?

56

How would your love life be different if you were your heroine for a month?

♥ Imagine what she would do with you, your love life, and your lifestyle.

♥ Now, consider following her example.

> To change your life, start immediately. Do it flamboyantly, no exceptions.
>
> William James

Do you ever think about how many adults stop going to classes, stop taking lessons, and stop playing sports once they graduate from high school or college and then wonder why their lives seem rather empty?

♥ Create a full life for yourself aside from your love life. You will be happier and you will be more interesting to others.

58

Do you ever think about totally starting over with your life?

♥ You could chuck it all and move!

♥ Billions of people on this planet don't know any of your history. It is never too late to begin anew.

59

How would an impartial third party view your love life?

♥ What would they say? What can you learn from this?

Do you ever think about how your life will be five years from now if you don't make some positive changes?

♥ Write out your dreams. Make a detailed plan regarding how to reach them. Then get to work.

♥ If you are really stuck in a rut, hire a life coach to work with you.

61

Do you ever ask your friends or family members to help you find Mr. Right?

♥ Many adults meet available singles through such channels.

♥ Blind dates do have good results for lots of singles.

62

Do you ever think that you are what you eat?

♥ You look better and feel better when you are eating healthy foods.

63

Do you believe that money equals power in relationships?

♥ The average woman still just earns seventy-six cents for every dollar a man earns.

♥ Have a financial strategy with your flame set up before you get married and be sure that you are comfortable with it.

If you must compromise, compromise up.

Eleanor Roosevelt

64

Do you ever think that if you haven't "been there" and "done that" by now that you might not get to unless you get busy?

Many women put their lives on hold until they meet a man, and they are just wasting some of the best years of their lives. Get out there and live your dreams whether you are married or not.

65

Do you ever think that once you get married you will have to say good-bye to dating forever?

 Is that a good thing to you or a bad thing? If you feel as if it is a bad thing, then maybe you aren't ready to settle down.

 However, don't forget to keep dating your spouse.

> Forget the times of your distress, but never forget what they taught you.
>
> Herbert Gasser

66

Do you ever think about what it would be like to date a celebrity?

♥ If the idea appeals to you, maybe you should consider getting yourself out in the limelight more.

67

What kind of man would you wish for if you knew that your fairy godmother would grant your wish?

♥ Do you usually date that kind of man?

♥ Is that type of man a healthy choice for you?

68

Are you looking for a sign to pursue a better love life?

♥ Maybe this is it. In your heart, you know what you want. Go after it. Take action to improve your life.

69

Do you ever think about your current flame's ex-girlfriend?

♥ Eighty-seven percent of women do admit to thinking about their boyfriend's old flames.

♥ The main concern is whether he is thinking of her.

Whom would you choose to date if you could pick absolutely anyone and you knew that he would be thrilled to date you?

💜 Ask yourself if he is within your reach. If so, go after him.

Let him have the key of thy heart who hath the lock of his own.

Sir Thomas Browne

71

Do you ever think about how your date has a friend and that friend has a friend?

♥ Watch your reputation carefully!

♥ If things don't work out with your original date, you may be introduced to someone wonderful through him.

♥ If things don't work out with your date romantically, you might still find a great friend.

Do you ever think about
how only 25 percent of
married people claim
to be happily married?

💜 Choose a partner wisely.

💜 An unhappy marriage can wreak havoc on
your life.

73

Do you think that dreams really do come true?

♥ Someone will win the lottery. Someone will win an Academy Award. Someone will become president of the United States. Someone's book will be number one on the bestseller list.

♥ Have faith. Don't give up on your dreams.

> You are never given a wish without also being given the power to make it come true.
>
> Richard Bach

Do you ever think about how your actions really do speak louder than your words?

💜 Are you nice to your dates?

💜 Are you on time?

💜 Are you flexible?

💜 Are you appreciative of the effort your date makes on your behalf?

💜 Do you dress your best?

💜 Are you fun?

Do you believe that there are unseen forces working on your behalf?

♥ Pray about your love life.

♥ Remember that miracles happen and that more things happen through prayer than we may even realize.

> Uncertainty and mystery are energies of life. Don't let them scare you unduly, for they keep boredom at bay and spark creativity.
>
> R. I. Fitzhenry

Do you ever think about
how it is easier to be nice
to someone and break it off
when you know that it won't
work than to lead someone
on and break his heart?

♥ Treat all dates the way you would want to be
treated.

77

What would it be like to talk
to your ten-year-old self,
your thirty-year-old self, and
your eighty-year-old self
regarding your love life?

♥ What would these wise creatures tell you?

♥ What can you learn from talking to them?

♥ Would they be proud of your love life or ashamed?

♥ What changes would they want you to make?

78

What type of impression do you make on others?

♥ What do women think of you?

♥ What do men think of you?

♥ Ask your friends and family for some feedback.

79

Do you believe that love is blind?

♥ It isn't, and the divorce statistics prove it.

Are you living to please
yourself or are you living
to please other people
with your love life?

The happiest people are those who follow their
own hearts.

Only the heart knows how
to find what is precious.
Fyodor Dostoyevsky

81

What do your nighttime dreams mean?

♥ What are you dreaming about your love life?

♥ Read a current self-help book on the meaning of dreams.

♥ Your nighttime dramas hold lots of helpful information for you to uncover.

82

Do you look forward to or dread the future?

♥ If you dread it, get to work and change it.

83

How would you define love, marriage, and romance?

♥ If you don't know what you are truly looking for, how will you ever find it?

♥ Define true romantic bliss so you will know what it means to you.

84

Would it take a miracle to fix your love life?

♥ More than 70 percent of American adults say they have experienced a miracle.

♥ Most Americans believe in miracles.

Do you ever think about your flame's background when you are considering a possible long-term relationship?

Eighty-five percent of males who experienced family violence during their teen years will be violent toward their spouses.

> Do what you can,
> with what you have,
> where you are.
>
> Theodore Roosevelt

86

Do you ever think about
how you have chosen the life
you have and that you could
change it for the better if
you really wanted to?

♥ Be brave and face the fact that you are respon-
sible for most of what goes on in your world.

♥ If you aren't happy, shake things up. Make positive changes.

87

Do you ever think about how your tall, dark, and handsome dream date might just turn into Mr. Bald and Overweight?

💜 Inner beauty lasts.

💜 Put more stock on what is inside than on what is on the outside.

💜 Look at the whole package and not just the wrapping.

88

Do you ever think about how women are four times more likely than men to live a good portion of their lives alone?

❤ Build a full life for yourself outside of your romantic life.

❤ Two-thirds of all women over age sixty-five are widows.

❤ If you want unconditional love throughout your adult life, always have a pet in your home.

> Our perfect companions never have fewer than four feet.
>
> Colette

Do you plan boring dates?

♥ Alan Caruba, head of the Boring Institute in Maplewood, New Jersey, lists the following as among the most boring of activities:

1. Meetings
2. Exercising
3. Housework
4. Political debates
5. Weeding

♥ Never plan a boring date if you want to have a successful love life.

90

Are you too shy in your approach to your love life?

♥ If shyness is a problem, get some help. Find a qualified therapist, read some self-help books on assertiveness, and resolve to take action.

91

Do you ever think about the role a good marriage plays in maintaining your health?

♥ According to a recent Harvard study of adult development, a happy marriage at age fifty is a better predictor of healthy aging than a low cholesterol level.

92

Do you ever think about how
you once played house and
what you expected male
and female roles to be?

❤ It might be a good time to check if you need to
update your expectations to prepare yourself
for a better future.

> Seize the moment.
> Remember all those women on
> the Titanic who waved off
> the dessert cart.
>
> Erma Bombeck

73

93

Do you ever think that the sermon you heard in church on Sunday might have been preached just for you?

💜 Are there any spiritual or ethical lessons you need to learn to help you with your love life?

94

How much or how little do you use your intuition?

💜 The more you use it, the better you will get at understanding your intuition.

Do you ever think about trying to organize a singles' event in your area?

♥ What do you have to lose?

♥ Lots of couples meet at singles' events.

♥ You might really enjoy organizing a special mixer, marathon, or charity event.

♥ Ask your single friends to help you and to bring along their single friends.

> Trust your hunches.
> Dr. Joyce Brothers

Would you choose the same friends you have today if you were picking new friends?

❤ It might be time to add some new friends to your social life.

❤ Keep in mind that new friends can add some sparkle to your social life.

❤ Female friends are a great buffer to the sometimes-harsh world of dating.

Do you ever think about adopting a dog or puppy from an animal shelter?

💜 Research suggests that singles with pets are happier than those without pets.

💜 Volunteering at an animal shelter can be a great way to meet people.

💜 Walking your dog or attending obedience classes and dog shows are wonderful ways to hobnob with other animal lovers of all backgrounds.

💜 Dogs provide safety and companionship for women living alone.

98

Do you ever think about calling your long-lost love?

♥ If you can't find him, check with family members or old friends.

♥ Check out all of the search engines on the Net to help you find him.

♥ Attend your next high school or college reunion.

The only menace is inertia.
St. John Perse

99

Do you ever think about how winners often do things that losers won't do?

💜 Be brave and go on a blind date.

💜 Try some new way of improving your love life.

💜 Join a dating service.

💜 Hire a professional matchmaker.

> I've been absolutely terrified
> every moment of my life, and I've never
> let it keep me from doing a single
> thing that I wanted to do.
>
> Georgia O'Keefe

Do you ever think when you are feeling sorry for yourself after a breakup or a bad date just how many tragedies haven't touched your life?

Count your blessings. You will be happier, and happy people are much more attractive to members of the opposite sex.

101

Do you ever think about going back to school?

♥ Adult education classes are one of the best places to meet men.

♥ Plus, it might help you with your career to continue your education.

In reality, we are still children. We want to find a playmate for our thoughts and feelings.

Dr. Wilhelm Stekhel

102

Do you use food as a source of comfort?

💜 Be careful if you answered yes to that question. Ninety-one percent of men say they would like to marry a woman with a good figure.

103

What were you like before your first broken heart?

💜 Have you grown from the experience, or have you allowed it to sour your point of view?

💜 It could be time to heal that broken heart if you haven't already.

Do you ever think about your friend's feelings when she is going through a dating dry spell and you aren't?

Jealousy is one of the main reasons that female friendships end. Tread lightly and consider her feelings when your love lives are out of sync.

Love is better than chocolate, but sometimes chocolate is easier to find.

Judy Kain

105

Do you ever think about the emotional baggage you might bring to a relationship?

♥ Fifty percent of girls living in a violent home will become a victim of partner abuse.

♥ If you have issues, seek professional help before you get involved with someone. That way the odds are much more in your favor to have a happy ending.

106

How would the great philosophers of old view your dating philosophy?

♥ Do you even know what your philosophy is?

♥ Discuss it with your friends to get a better understanding of your whole viewpoint.

107

Do you ever think about going on an adventure or trying some exciting new activity?

♥ Even if you don't meet Mr. Right, you will shake up your world a bit and have some fun.

What love-life regrets might you have if you don't take action?

💜 Make a list of possible regrets.

💜 Are there any steps that you might want to take?

💜 Talk with a trusted friend about taking some action.

It is a bad plan that
can't be changed.

Publilius Syrus

109

Do you ever think about how you can add a little special romantic touch to your life even though you are single?

♥ Buy yourself a pretty nightgown.

♥ Send yourself some flowers.

♥ Give yourself a box of yummy chocolates.

♥ Wear wonderful perfume.

♥ Sleep on satin sheets.

♥ Listen to a romantic CD.

♥ Burn scented candles.

Do you ever think about the amount of effort you put into your love life?

💜 How many new men do you meet during the course of a week?

💜 Do you belong to any clubs or volunteer for any charities?

💜 Do you get out and about, or are you a homebody?

💜 Are you positive in your outlook?

111

Do you ever think about
what your life would be
like if you had an identical
twin and how she would
handle her love life?

♥ Can you learn anything from your imaginary
sister?

Success is dependent
on effort.

Sophocles

Do you ever think about creating special romantic memories for your girlfriends and their dates?

💜 It will get your romantic juices flowing.

💜 Your friends will appreciate your efforts.

💜 They might just return the favor.

Desire and hope will push us
on toward the future.

Michael de Montaigne

113

What three words would most people use to describe your personality?

♥ Ask your friends and family for their best description of you. Do you like what you hear? If not, get to work on some self-improvement.

114

Do you pamper yourself?

♥ What would that mean to you?

♥ Make yourself feel special, for it will come across to others that you are indeed an important, wonderful woman.

115

Do you ever think about writing the story of your life?

♥ Who would play you in the movie version of your book?

♥ Who would play your love interests?

♥ Can you learn anything from these characters?

♥ Is the book a tearjerker or a happily-ever-after story?

> We create our fate every day....
> Most of the ills we suffer
> from are directly traceable
> to our own behavior.
>
> Henry Miller

Do you ever think about how many little decisions you make in a day and that if you made different choices, your life would be different?

 For the next ten days try a little experiment and do many of your day-to-day routines a bit differently.

 Go to new places at different times with different people, and watch how your life expands.

 You might just improve your love life.

 You will feel more alive.

117

Are you a high- or low-maintenance woman?

♥ The majority of women say they fall in between.

♥ The vast majority of men say they would like to marry a low-maintenance woman.

118

Do you ever think about the times when you were a child and looked up to adults?

♥ What lessons were you learning about men and women?

♥ Do those lessons need to be updated?

119

Do you ever think about those wonderful times when you wanted to stay awake to watch for Santa or the Easter Bunny?

💜 How long has it been since you were that happy and excited?

💜 What could you do to bring some magic back into your life?

> There are no rules.
> Just follow your heart.
>
> Robin Williams

120

Do you ever worry about getting into hot water with your current boyfriend?

♥ What behavior gets you into trouble and why?

♥ Is your boyfriend out of line, or do you need to straighten up a bit?

Draw your strength from who you are.

Russell Means

121

Do you ever think about those times long ago when your love-life dreams were brand new?

♥ How have they changed? Did they change for the better or worse?

122

Do you ever think about how your time and attention are priceless to your significant other?

♥ Give yourself credit for the important role you play in other peoples' lives.

123

Do you ever think about
exercising on a date if you
or your significant other
is a fitness buff?

More and more singles are joining health clubs
and many couples enjoy working out together.

Or, you can join a gym and perhaps meet a
great guy while you get healthier.

Do you ever think about those days when Saturdays were made just for play dates and not for romantic dates?

♥ Why not take a weekend or two off from the dating world and give yourself a break? The dating scene might seem a little less like work if you have had some really good girl time.

Now for some heart work.
Rainer Maria Rilke

125

Do you make the effort to attend all or at least most of the events that are important to your significant other?

💜 How many of his games have you attended?

💜 Do you bail out of family events?

💜 Do you attend his company's parties?

Do you ever think about pampering yourself at a spa for a weekend?

💜 If you don't take good care of yourself, who will?

💜 You might clear out some emotional cobwebs by getting out of your normal routine and make yourself a lot happier in the process.

💜 Try a visit to a coed spa and you just might meet Mr. Right while you are getting away from the world.

127

Do you ever think about all of the things you know intuitively about your date's personality?

💜 Do you like what you know?

💜 Pay attention to your inner whisperings.

128

Do you compare your current beau to your old boyfriends?

💜 Why do you do it?

💜 Can any man ever stack up to your old images?

129

Are you holding any grudges against specific members of the opposite sex or against the male species in general?

💜 Forty-four percent of women admit to having negative feelings about the opposite sex after a romantic breakup.

💜 The more emotional garbage you can identify and get rid of before you get into a romantic relationship, the better your chances are for success.

130

Do you understand all of the developmental stages of romantic relationships?

💜 The first is the getting-to-know-each-other stage.

💜 The second involves the growth of feelings and affection.

💜 The third stage is a period of significant learning about the other person's life.

💜 The fourth stage is a period of increased or decreased affection.

💜 The final period is when couples decide to continue or end the relationship.

Do you have a forgiving heart?

💜 What does it take to cross your bottom line in a relationship?

💜 Do you bail out too soon, or should you throw the bums out earlier?

💜 Ask your friends for their input.

> There are years that ask questions and years that answer.
>
> Zora Neale Hurston

What are your needs, wants, and desires outside of your love life?

♥ What other areas of your life hold your attention and passion?

♥ Maybe you are not giving the other areas in your life enough attention.

♥ Make a pie chart of all of the areas of your life and see where you are spending your time and energy.

♥ Is your life off balance?

Do you set aside a certain amount of time to concentrate on the spiritual side of your life?

♥ Isn't that the real reason you are here in the first place?

♥ Could it be that if you got that area into its proper focus then just maybe the rest of your life might come together?

> Perhaps if one really knew when one was happy one would know the things that were necessary for one's life.
>
> Joanna Field

Do you live in the present moment or are you wasting it thinking about the past or future?

💜 Sixty-two percent of women claim they spend much of their present relationship concerned with questions about the future of the relationship.

💜 Do you think that you might be better off letting the relationship just happen and taking it day by day?

💜 Why waste the present worrying about what might or might not happen?

Do you ever think about whether you should be giving out more compliments and less criticism to your dates?

💜 Keep track on your next few dates of how many negative and positive things you say.

💜 What is your score?

💜 Remember that people love to hear good things about themselves.

> Love is a gross exaggeration of the difference between one person and everybody else.
>
> George Bernard Shaw

How much do you really know about your current love interest's friends, family, and coworkers?

💜 Do you feel that he is private or open?

💜 Do you feel that he is honest or shading the truth?

💜 Are you comfortable with what you hear and observe?

💜 Do you need to ask more questions?

💜 Are you afraid of the truth, or does it make you uncomfortable?

💜 Are you avoiding certain subjects in your conversations? Why?

137

How would you be feeling if you knew that today was your last day on earth?

💜 How do your feelings change regarding your love life?

💜 Who is really important to you?

138

What are your dog's feelings about your current beau?

💜 Eighty-two percent of dog owners claim that their pooches are good judges of character.

139

What embarrasses you the most about yourself?

♥ Do you need to make some changes?

♥ Should you be easier on yourself?

140

Are you enjoying your love life?

♥ If not, stir things up. Take some risks. Make some changes. Have some fun.

141

If you were your mother,
what would you want
for your little girl in the
love-life department?

♥ Moms usually want the best for their daughters.
Are you settling for less?

♥ Try to detach and see your dates through her
eyes. What do you see?

♥ Are the men in your life princes or black knights
in your mom's eyes?

The greatest deceiver—
one who deceives himself.

Dr. Frank Crane

Do you ever think about getting rid of the energy drains in your life to make room for more positive things to come in?

💜 What do you find trying in your life?

💜 How hard would it be to get rid of these energy drains or at least to lessen their impact on you?

When we bury feelings, we also bury ourselves.

Nathaniel Branden

143

Do you ever think about what your friends are learning about dating and men from watching your love life?

💜 Are you a positive role model?

💜 Do your friends think that men are wonderful or evil from observing your boyfriends?

> Character is what a man is in the dark.
> Dwight L. Moody

144

Do you ever think about when you were little and worried about monsters in the dark?

💜 What monsters do you worry about when you go to bed now?

💜 Are you afraid of growing old alone? Eighty-four percent of singles say that they worry about this.

Follow your inner moonlight.

Allen Ginsberg

145

Are you on time for dates, or do you make men wait for you to get ready?

♥ In a recent survey, single men complained that being kept waiting was one of their biggest pet peeves of dating.

146

How long a time frame do you like to plan between a first and second date?

♥ The majority of singles like to have no more than a week between dates.

147

Do you ever think about how you would feel if your future child turned out to be a carbon copy of your current beau?

♥ Does that thought bring you great joy or great sorrow?

148

How does your handshake feel to others?

♥ Eighty-three percent of singles state that a wimpy handshake means that the person lacks confidence.

149

Are your images of love and romance that of an adult or of a child?

💜 Ask your friends for their input.

💜 The more mature your thoughts about love are, the more likely you will be able to maintain a healthy, happy relationship.

> We have to challenge the status quo to allow for a better future.
>
> Samuel Mockbee

150

Do your dates see you smiling, laughing, and happy a lot, or are you showing them the opposite side of your personality?

♥ Optimism was one of the top five characteristics that single men claimed they valued most in a future mate.

♥ Practice looking on the bright side of life. You will be happier and you will be more attractive to members of the opposite sex.

♥ Remember that positive people also enjoy better health than their sour counterparts.

151

Did you know that if you smoke, the majority of single men will immediately be turned off?

In a recent study of single men between the ages of twenty-one and thirty-five, more than 60 percent stated that they would not want to date a woman who is a heavy smoker.

> It is a sad day when you find out that it's not accident or time or fortune but just yourself that kept things from you.
>
> Lillian Hellman

15²

Do you ever think that your date's point of view might just be correct even though it differs from yours?

You can always learn from others and the gift of empathy and understanding are wonderful traits to possess to ensure marital bliss.

Let your soul stand cool and composed before a million universes.

Walt Whitman

153

Do you apologize when you make a dating faux pas?

♥ Many singles try to ignore their blunder, but many mistakes can be quickly erased if one admits the error and apologizes immediately.

154

Do you ask God your dating questions?

♥ What better authority could there be?

Do you ever think about how it is easier to build a healthy relationship with someone than to try to repair an unhealthy relationship?

♥ Watch what you say and do and make smart decisions regarding your behavior.

♥ Keep in mind that your actions always have consequences.

♥ You really do reap what you sow.

What one love-life memento would you rescue if your home caught on fire?

💜 Who is it from?

💜 What is the significance to you?

> It seems to me that our three basic needs, for food and security and love, are so entwined that we cannot think of one without the other.
>
> M.F.K. Fisher

What would your guardian angel say about your love life?

♥ Is it spiritually based?

♥ Do you practice the golden rule?

♥ Are you a role model for friends and family?

♥ Are the men you date better off for having known you?

♥ Are you the kind of woman who makes other women feel good about their gender?

What specific thing about your love life brings you the most happiness?

💜 Is it having someone to share activities with?

💜 Is it the security of being a couple?

💜 Is it the excitement of the chase?

💜 If you can answer this question, you might just be one step closer to understanding what you need most from a romantic relationship.

> More things are wrought by prayer than this world dreams of.
>
> Alfred, Lord Tennyson

Did Cinderella and Snow White influence your idea of romance?

More than 40 percent of girls in the United States have either seen these movies or read these stories.

All you need is deep within you waiting to unfold and reveal itself. All you have to do is be still and take time to seek for what is within, and you will surely find it.

Eileen Caddy

How much time would you like to spend with your mate once you get married?

💜 The average married person in the United States talks less than ten minutes a day with their mate.

💜 How does that sobering statistic make you feel?

💜 What could you and your mate do to keep the romance and friendship alive?

Do you ever think about going public with your search for Mr. Right?

💜 Ask neighbors and coworkers to keep you in mind for a fun set-up.

💜 Check with your siblings and their friends for available singles.

💜 Consider asking your parents to set you up with their friends' children.

💜 Look around any clubs you belong to and ask fellow members for some introductions to members you haven't gotten to know who are also single.

Do you keep your love life in balance, or do you go off the deep end every time you begin a new relationship?

💜 Moderation is key.

💜 Relax and take things slowly.

💜 Real love grows over time, while infatuations die out.

> All significant battles
> are waged within the self.
>
> Sheldon Kopp

Do you ever think about hiring a life coach?

♥ Many singles are gaining some important tips by working with a qualified, objective professional.

♥ What do you have to lose by trying a bit of coaching?

> Learning what's going on inside you can be difficult, but it's also invigorating, and the rewards are enormous.
>
> Barbara Sher

Do you ever think about how you spend your money?

♥ Where does it all go?

♥ How much do you actually spend on dating?

♥ Should you rework your budget to allow for more entertaining or traveling?

♥ Is your budget realistic regarding your love-life goals?

♥ Can you afford to join a club that might allow you to meet some great singles?

♥ Should you spend more on your wardrobe and grooming? Keep in mind that first impressions do matter in the dating world.

165

Do you ever think about how your significant other spends his money?

♥ Are your financial styles compatible?

♥ Married couples list finances as the number one area of disagreement.

♥ What does money mean to you?

♥ What does money represent to your significant other?

> For where your treasure is, there will your heart be also.
>
> Matthew 6:21

166

Do you ever think about your breath?

♥ Singles claim that bad breath is reason enough not to go on a second date with someone.

♥ Check your breath, and if you have a problem that mouthwash and breath mints won't solve, consult your dentist or doctor.

167

Do you ever think about the fact that men gossip?

♥ A recent study suggests that there are no differences between the sexes in the quantity of time spent gossiping.

168

Do you ever think about
how your beau will handle
the biggest shopping
day of the year, the day
after Thanksgiving?

💜 Is he a shopper?

💜 Are you?

💜 Are your gift-giving budgets compatible?

136

Do you ever think about how opposites attract, but then they often begin to irritate each other with their differences?

💜 Do you admire the differences you see in your significant other, or are you planning to change him in the near future?

💜 Can you learn from the differences between you two, or are they future battles waiting to happen?

170

Do you ever think about why opposites attract?

♥ We envy what we don't have.

♥ People who are different from ourselves are often viewed as exciting and even mysterious.

> Let me remember that each life must follow its own course, and that what happens to other people has absolutely nothing to do with what happens to me.
>
> Marjorie Holmes

171

Do you ever dream of marrying a doctor?

♥ There are just over 710,000 male doctors in the United States.

♥ This is the number-one profession that women state is desirable in a potential mate.

172

Do you ever think about how well you really know yourself?

♥ The better you understand yourself, the more likely you will be to create and maintain a loving relationship with a romantic partner.

173

Do you believe in luck?

♥ What makes you feel lucky?

♥ Can you empower yourself through using your lucky charms and rituals?

174

Do you believe that there is only one soul mate for you?

♥ This belief will certainly limit your love life.

175

Do you understand that the harder you work at something, the "luckier" you become?

Are you working hard on having a good love life?

Could you work a bit harder?

> We find what we search for—or, if we don't find it, we become it.
>
> Jessamyn West

176

What does your dad think about your love life?

💜 Does he like the men you date?

💜 Are they like your dad?

💜 Is he proud of your morals?

💜 Would your dad and your significant other be pals if you married?

💜 What type of relationship does your dad want with the men in your life?

Do you ever think about your lowest love-life moments?

💜 Do you play those moments over and over again in your mind?

💜 Are you beating yourself up over those experiences or have your learned your lessons and moved on?

💜 What do those moments have in common?

💜 Were all of those moments with the same person or different people?

💜 Are they recent memories or moments rooted in the far past?

💜 Were these low points preventable? If so, how can you stop them from happening in the future?

What do women's rights mean to you?

💜 What impact do they have on your love life?

💜 Do you ever play second fiddle to a man?

💜 Do you feel equal to men?

> So many women just don't know how great they are. They come to us all vogue on the outside and vague on the inside.
>
> Mary Kay Ash

179

When you marry, will you take your husband's last name or keep your own last name?

♥ More than 90 percent of women take their husband's last name when they get married.

♥ What special circumstances would have to happen to make you change your view?

180

Do you ever think about the ideal age to marry?

♥ Studies suggest that your chances for having a happy marriage will improve if you wait until you are past twenty-three years old to marry.

181

Do you ever think about how change is a part of life?

♥ You won't always be dating.

♥ You won't always be single.

♥ You won't always be falling in and out of love.

♥ You won't always be young.

> It's never too late in fiction or in life to revise.
> Nancy Thayer

182

Do you ever lie about your love life?

💜 Why do you feel the need to stretch or change the truth?

💜 Are you embarrassed?

💜 Are you ashamed?

💜 Who do you lie to and why?

> Since we cannot change reality, let us change the eyes which see reality.
>
> Nikos Kazantzakis

183

How you would define your "type"?

♥ Do you really date your type?

♥ Is your type a good choice for you, or should you update your definition of the perfect guy for you?

♥ Would your type be drawn to a woman like you?

184

Do you ever settle for less than you deserve?

♥ Always try to grab the best for yourself.

♥ Believe that you deserve happiness and love.

185

Do you ever think about how much money the men in your life spend on dating you?

💜 Are they frugal or wild and crazy spenders?

💜 Are you happy with their spending habits?

💜 Are you reasonable in your expectations?

The "weaker sex" is the stronger sex because of the weakness of the stronger sex for the weaker sex.

UNKNOWN

Do you ever think about
the fact that more men
than women report serious
pre-wedding jitters?

Could it be that it is more socially acceptable for
men to show their fear of giving up their inde-
pendence?

Listening to your heart
is not simple. Finding out who you
are is not simple. It takes a lot of
hard work and courage to get to know
who you are and what you want.

Sue Bender

187

When do you think is the best time to have a wedding?

♥ More couples marry in June than in any other month.

♥ The term "June Bride" brings images of happy summer days to many couples.

188

How resourceful are you when it comes to meeting available singles?

♥ Rate yourself on a scale from one to ten. If you fall below a six, brainstorm some new ways to meet other singles.

How much of your self-esteem is wrapped up in your love life?

♥ Is that hurting or helping your self-esteem?

♥ Base your self-esteem on who you are as a person and not on who you do or do not date.

> Always be a first-rate version of yourself instead of a second-rate version of somebody else.
>
> Judy Garland

190

Do you ever think about
the fact that every marriage
goes through an adjustment
period and not straight to the
happily-ever-after part?

♥ Be sure to base your idea of marriage on reality
and not on some silly, romantic fairy-tale
version of reality.

191

Do you and your significant other travel in the same social circles?

💜 Do you like each other's friends?

💜 Are you comfortable in each other's worlds?

> We marry for all the wrong reasons, and often we marry the wrong person as well...we marry to grow up, to escape our parents, and to inherit our share of the world, not knowing who we are and who we will become.
>
> Merle Shain

192

Do you ever think about changing yourself to please a man?

♥ Eighty percent of married women say they believe that married women submerge a vital part of themselves when they marry.

> Womankind suffers from three delusions: marriage will reform a man; a rejected lover is heartbroken for life; and if the other woman were only out of the way he would come back.
>
> Myrtle Reed

193

Would you recognize the five signs of marital dissatisfaction?

♥ They are adultery, depression, addiction, physical abuse, and emotional abuse.

♥ Women are twice as likely to become depressed over a bad marriage than men are.

194

Do you ever think about how the majority of divorces are filed by women?

♥ Up until the last two decades, men filed more frequently for divorce.

What does your jewelry say about you?

💗 Do you project a fun or flirty style?

💗 Are you fashion-forward or traditional?

💗 Do you favor expensive pieces or inexpensive imitations?

💗 Do you wear a ring on the third finger of your left hand? If so, you may be scaring off men who might think you are married.

💗 Does your jewelry make any political statement?

💗 Does your jewelry represent the inner you?

Do you ever think about how the great romantics of all time lived and loved?

❤ In your mind, who are these people?

❤ What can you learn from them?

❤ Were they happily married or always playing the field?

> Our life always expresses the result of our dominant thoughts.
>
> Soren Kierkegaard

197

Are you good marriage material?

♥ Ask members of the opposite sex what they think. You might be in for a big shock.

♥ Refrain from asking your dates this question or they may think that you are trying to push the relationship.

198

Are you an inner-directed or outer-directed person regarding your love life?

♥ The happiest people are those who are inner directed.

199

How will you feel when your mate spends the money you earn?

 Are you good at sharing?

 Do you have a financial plan for your marriage?

 Is it reasonable?

Do you ever look at your love life through the eyes of detachment?

💜 How does it look?

💜 What role do you play?

💜 Is it a happy tale?

> your vision will become clear only when you look into your heart...who looks outside, dreams. Who looks inside, awakens.
>
> Carl Young

Do you ever think about changing your appearance with cosmetic surgery?

❤ In 1999, four hundred thousand Americans had liposuction.

❤ In other words, we are a very beauty-conscious society.

❤ The number of men who are opting for cosmetic surgery is growing every year.

202

Do you ever think about
what your life and marriage
would have looked like at the
turn of the last century?

In 1890, only 2 percent of women had jobs outside of the home.

Hold fast to your
illusions—they'll keep
you young and happy.

UNKNOWN

203

Do you ever justify your dating behavior to others?

💜 Why?

💜 Are you making bad choices?

💜 Are your friends not supportive?

💜 Are you not living up to your potential?

> Many women today feel a sadness we cannot name. Though we accomplish much of what we set out to do, we sense that something is missing in our lives and—fruitlessly—search "out there" for the answers. What's often wrong is that we are disconnected from an authentic sense of self.
>
> Emily Hancock

164

What brings you resolution after an argument with your significant other?

💜 Seventy-five percent of women say that sharing their feelings gives them closure.

💜 Sixty-seven percent of men say that sharing a fun activity brings them a sense of closure.

205

Do you ever think about the fact that an exercise program will increase your self-esteem?

💜 It will also make you healthier!

206

How many irritating qualities do you have?

💜 If you think that you don't have any, check with a few trusted friends.

💜 It could be that you just might need to do a little clean-up act on your behavior to be more appealing to members of the opposite sex.

How much time do you spend dreaming of getting that diamond ring on your left hand?

♥ Give yourself a break, and buy yourself some diamond earrings in the meantime.

> Five years from now you will be pretty much the same as you are today except for two things: the books you read and the people you get close to.
>
> Charles Jones

Does pride keep you from buying items that might help your love life?

💜 Shop online for self-help books if you feel uncomfortable buying them at your local bookstore.

💜 There has been a 50 percent increase in online shopping just in the last year.

> True love is like ghosts, which everybody talks about and few have seen.
>
> Franwois de la Rochefoucauld

209

Do you ever play emotional games when you are involved in a romantic relationship?

💜 Remember that honesty is the best policy.

💜 Game playing just leads to more game playing.

💜 You want to be loved for the real you and not because you played some emotional head game with your significant other.

210

Do you ever think about how healthy commitments come from the heart and not from being forced?

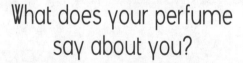

Ultimatums can easily backfire.

211

What does your perfume say about you?

Does it match your style?

Do you change fragrances, or do you have a trademark scent?

Do you ever think about having a long-distance romance?

💜 The majority of singles say they have been involved in at least one long-distance love affair.

💜 The use of email has increased the temptation of becoming romantically involved with a far-away lover.

It is the individual who knows how little he knows about himself who stands a reasonable chance of finding out something about himself.

S.I. Hayakawa

Do you ever think about how there are three sides to a relationship?

💜 Your side.

💜 His side.

💜 Reality.

> Some things have to be believed to be seen.
>
> Ralph Hodgson

Did you know the vast majority of women say that they prefer cuddling to sex?

💜 Can you understand how this can cause problems in a marriage?

💜 Are you prepared to deal with this conflict since the majority of men prefer sex to cuddling once you marry?

> Men are like cellophane—
> transparent, but hard to
> remove once you get
> wrapped up in them.
>
> UNKNOWN

How does your home appear to your dates?

💜 Is it clean and tidy?

💜 Is it nicely decorated?

💜 Does it reflect your personality?

💜 Do you have pictures of old flames around?

💜 Are your pets well groomed and well mannered?

💜 Do old loves drop over uninvited?

216

What would you do if your friend's significant other came on to you?

♥ More than 60 percent of women say that this has happened to them.

217

Do you ever think about what day of the week you want to get married on?

♥ The vast majority of weddings take place on Saturday.

Do you ever think about how your choice of a roommate affects your date's opinion of you?

♥ Is your roommate nice to your dates?

♥ Is she or he presentable?

♥ Do you live with members of the opposite sex? If so, could that be hurting your love life?

219

Do you ever think about using the wonders of nature to enhance your love life?

💜 Try putting the following to work for you:

> Full moon
>
> Star-filled nights
>
> Rainbow to wish upon
>
> Beautiful scenery
>
> Flowers that smell sweet and romantic
>
> The sound of waves crashing on a shore
>
> New moon to wish upon

220

Do you ever think about how many states are now requiring premarital counseling?

💜 What are the laws in your state?

💜 What do you think you could learn through counseling?

💜 Would you want to go for premarital counseling even if your state didn't require it?

221

Do you ever think about
how your spouse should
come before your parents
and friends on your
list of priorities?

Can your parents deal with that, or will you need
to walk them through that life change?

To cheat oneself out of love
is the most terrible deception. It is
an eternal loss for which there is
no reparation. Either in time
or in eternity.

Soren Kierkegaard

179

Do you ever think about the fact that the healthiest reason to get married is that you have found the right person?

💜 Many people marry for the wrong reasons and end up in divorce court because of it.

💜 The worst reasons for marrying include:

1. All of your friends are getting married.

2. You are tired of dating.

3. You want to feel grown up.

4. Your old flame just got married.

5. You want to start a family, and your biological clock is ticking loudly.

223

Do you handle first dates well?

💜 Many people get very nervous on first dates.

💜 Consider a double date if your dating nerves get the best of you. Surrounding yourself with friends can help you to relax.

💜 Exercise before a first date to get rid of dating jitters.

💜 Meditate before a first date to get yourself into the right frame of mind.

Ever forward, but slowly.

Gebhard Leberecht von Blucher

224

Do you ever think about how much money you have spent on gifts for former boyfriends?

 Do you now wish that you hadn't been so generous?

 The average married couple spends $483 a year on gifts for each other.

225

Do you take relationships slowly enough, or do you always jump right in?

♥ Remember the old adage of slow and steady wins the race.

226

Do you ever think about having children?

♥ Sixty-eight percent of single adults say that they want to have children.

227

Do you ever think about why you date?

♥ Are you looking for fun and friendship?

♥ Or are you looking for a mate?

♥ Do you just date to have a companion for social events?

> The secret of happiness
> is in getting what you want—
> not what you want others
> to think you want.
>
> UNKNOWN

What are your feelings regarding prenuptial agreements?

💜 Will you ask your significant other to sign one?

💜 Would you be willing to sign one?

💜 How would you feel if your significant other wouldn't marry you unless you signed a prenup?

> Everyone, without exception, is searching for happiness.
>
> Blaise Pascal

How would your love life change if you won the lottery?

❤ Would you dump your current beau?

❤ Would you still want to marry in the near future?

❤ How would your new finances change your hobbies and entertaining style?

❤ How would you change your dating life?

> I have no home but me.
> Anne Truitt

230

Do you ever lose your temper on dates?

♥ Are you too angry?

♥ Or do you not stand up for yourself enough with members of the opposite sex?

> Let go of the people who cause constant pain; let go of the negativity that colors a room more darkly than any coat of paint. Keep close the people you love, the ones who stay engaged and open to life, who bring joy and peace to the house and garden.
>
> Dominique Browning

231

Do you believe that romantic love is unconditional?

It shouldn't be. You should not accept abuse from your partner in the name of love!

232

Do you believe that love is fair?

Studies show that people who believe that life is fair also believe that love is fair.

233

How have the television
programs you watched
growing up impacted
your view of marriage?

💜 Do you think that you should be Mrs. Brady or
Roseanne Barr?

💜 What shows did you like?

💜 What character did you relate to?

💜 Who influenced your views the most?

Do you ever think about the overall quality of your voice?

💜 Is it too nasal?

💜 Is it pleasing?

💜 Does it sound strong and confident?

💜 Do you whine?

💜 If you need a little improvement, consider working with a voice coach or a speech teacher.

235

What is your love life teaching your children if you are a single parent?

♥ Remember your first responsibility is to them.

♥ Keep in mind that you are your children's greatest role model.

> Love is the wisdom of the fool and the folly of the wise.
>
> Samuel Johnson

How many members of the opposite sex do you have as friends?

💜 Are you more of a buddy to males instead of being a romantic partner?

💜 Do you have lots of male friends? You can learn a lot from them regarding your love life.

💜 Male friends are a great resource for other available men.

💜 Your female friends would probably love it if you set them up with your great male friends, and get your friends to return the favor!

What is your philosophy regarding who should pay on the first date?

♥ The easiest rule to follow is that the one who asks for the date is usually the one who pays.

♥ Always carry some cash on your dates to cover dating expenses in case your date thinks that you are going to pay.

♥ Men generally pay for all of the first few dates.

♥ Younger men are more comfortable than men over thirty-five with women paying for the dates.

♥ Men in urban settings are more comfortable with women paying than men in rural areas.

Do you think about the median age for men and women getting married?

💜 The median age for men is 26.8.

💜 The median age for women is 25.1.

💜 How old do you want to be when you dream of your perfect wedding?

It is never too late to be what you might have been.

George Eliot

Do your friends want the very best for you?

♥ Surround yourself with people who truly have your best interests at heart.

♥ Stay away from "friends" who are jealous and petty.

> The key is to keep company only with people who uplift you, whose presence calls forth your best.
>
> Epictetus

Do you ever think about the deep meaning of your dreams regarding your significant other?

💜 Are they happy?

💜 Do you get a sense of danger?

💜 Do you have a recurring theme?

💜 What messages do you receive in your dreams?

Do you ever judge men too harshly?

💜 Do you judge yourself too harshly?

💜 Ask your friends if you are too tough on the men in your life.

💜 Could it be that you aren't giving people the benefit of the doubt?

> Even the most ordinary life is a mystery if you look close enough.
>
> Kennedy Fraser

How will your social life change in the next five or ten years?

♥ Do you like the changes that you envision for yourself?

♥ If you don't like those changes, try rewriting the script you have written for your life.

Marriage is like a tourniquet; it stops your circulation.

UNKNOWN

Do you ever think about hiring a professional matchmaker?

♥ Many people pay thousands of dollars to professional matchmakers to find them a great match.

♥ Professional matchmakers can be found in many large urban settings.

♥ Use caution when choosing a matchmaker. Check references and the Better Business Bureau.

Would you be a better employee if you were married?

Eighty percent of managers believe that married employees are better workers and more reliable than their single counterparts.

He who love touches not walks in darkness.

Plato

Why do you want to get married?

♥ The number one reason people give for wanting to get married is love.

♥ The number two reason is to escape loneliness.

♥ The third reason is that people feel a sense of social pressure to marry after a certain age.

Does alcohol make you feel or behave differently toward your significant other?

💜 Do you like him more or less? Why?

💜 Does alcohol make you feel differently toward men in general?

> A false enchantment can last a lifetime.
>
> W.H. Auden

Do you ever think about what you would do if your best friend's date wanted to date you instead of your friend?

💜 Would you be loyal? The majority of women claim that they would be loyal to their friend.

💜 Most women say that if he cheated on their friend, then he would cheat on them, too. They say a man isn't worth losing a female friend over.

When people show you who they are, believe them.

Maya Angelou

248

What color is your aura?

💙 Is it one of a highly developed individual, or is it all dark and dreary?

💙 Do you even believe that people have auras?

249

Do you ever think about what your significant other will be like in later years?

💙 Will he be a jolly old man, or do you picture him as a mean old grump?

250

Do you ever think about the importance of patience when it comes to love?

💜 Remember that good things often do come to those who wait.

💜 True love takes time.

> People change and forget to tell each other.
> Lillian Hellman

251

Do you present your achievements proudly to your love interests, or do you hide behind false modesty?

❤ Winners are attracted to other winners.

❤ Put your best foot forward.

> Winners are those people who make a habit of doing things losers are uncomfortable doing.
>
> Ed Foreman

252

Do you ever think about how recent studies suggest that one-third of all current jobs will change dramatically in the next five years?

♥ How might that affect your love life?

♥ Should you be getting more training now while you are single and have more free time?

Change creates movement; movement creates change.

Jerry Downs

253

Do you keep your commitments to others?

♥ You are constantly building your reputation, so be sure to honor all of your commitments.

254

Do you appear desperate to members of the opposite sex?

♥ If you feel desperate, you are very likely to appear desperate.

Do you ever think about your taste in music?

💜 Do you listen to upbeat songs, or are you drawn to sad love songs?

💜 Could it be time to choose an upbeat theme song?

💜 You can change your mood by changing the type of music that you listen to.

> In solitude we give passionate attention to our lives, to our memories, to the details around us.
>
> Virginia Woolf

Do you ever think about how much time you have left in this life?

♥ The lifespan for the average man is seventy-two years.

♥ The lifespan for the average woman is seventy-seven years.

> We are all visitors on this planet....During this period we must try to do something good, something useful with our lives.
>
> Dalai Lama

257

Are you drawn to men who have the qualities that you value but lack?

♥ What are those values?

♥ Work on developing them in yourself instead of just looking for them in a mate.

258

Where do you go to meet singles?

♥ Would the type of mate you want to attract be likely to go there?

How do your financial and social status affect your love life?

💜 Are you affected in a positive or negative way?

💜 What positive changes could you implement?

💜 Are you willing to date men from a different status level?

> Age doesn't protect you from love. But love, to some extent, protects you from age.
>
> Jeanne Moreau

260

What role does your age play in your romantic expectations?

♥ Research suggests that women become more discerning after age twenty-five but less discerning after age forty.

261

What would life be like if you marry a sports nut and you don't like sports?

♥ Many women claim to be football widows, and this brings on lots of resentment.

What household chores would you expect your mate to perform?

♥ The average woman still does four times as much housework as her spouse.

How does your significant other feel about household chores?

♥ What are his expectations regarding household responsibilities?

♥ Look at his parents' division of labor to get an idea of what he might expect.

264

Do you ever become defensive during disagreements?

♥ How could you remain more open?

265

How would you feel if your significant other became disabled?

♥ More men than women say that they would end the relationship because they couldn't deal with such a serious situation.

Does your current love interest cause you to feel less satisfied with your life?

❤ A quality relationship should make you feel happier in life.

Behavior is a mirror in which everyone shows his image.

Johann Wolfgang von Goethe

267

Do you ever take a ten-minute breather before you begin an argument with your significant other?

Sometimes a little break can help you see things more clearly.

If you are prone to having a temper tantrum, a break can calm your nerves and prevent you from saying things that you might regret.

Eighty-two percent of singles admit to saying things to a love interest in anger that they regret.

268

Do you ever think about
the type of woman who
would appeal to the man
of your dreams?

♥ Do you fit that description?

♥ If not, do you want to make some changes?
Would those be positive changes for you? If not,
why would you want to make those changes?

> She listens to her own
> tales, laughs at her own jokes,
> and follows her own advice.
>
> Ama Ata Aidoo

269

Do you ever think about the fact that you have only a 10 percent chance of marrying someone who is left handed?

Ninety percent of the American population is right handed.

As one goes through life, one learns that if you don't paddle your own canoe, you don't move.

Katharine Hepburn

270

Are you a top priority for your significant other?

♥ If not, why have you allowed him to be so important to you?

271

Do you dig up the past whenever you argue with your current mate?

♥ Resolve past conflicts and then move forward.

♥ Let bygones be bygones.

Do you nip problems in the bud when they start in your romantic relationships instead of letting them drag on and on?

♥ Are you afraid of conflict?

♥ Do you hang on to relationships long after you know the man isn't right for you?

♥ Are you guilty of being too nice?

> Each relationship you have with another person reflects the relationship you have with yourself.
>
> Alice Deville

273

Do you ever stereotype men?

♥ You can miss out on some wonderful friends and partners by making snap judgments.

274

Do you try too hard to please men?

♥ The vast majority of college students list trying too hard as the number one turn-off for potential dates.

♥ Relax. Be yourself. It will either work out or you will be better off with someone else.

275

Do you ever think about how real love is energizing?

♥ Research shows that couples in love require less sleep.

♥ People who claim to be in love also get fewer colds.

> Love is the only way to grasp another human being in the innermost core of his personality.
>
> Viktor Frankl

Did you know that married men fantasize about their single days while married women don't seem to miss those days nearly as much?

♥ However, research shows that married men are generally happier than married women.

♥ Could it be that married women just don't admit to missing their single days for fear of hurting their mate's feelings?

It may be those who do the least, dream the most.

UNKNOWN

277

Do you ever think that
possessiveness is one
of the biggest turn-offs
for both sexes?

♥ Give your significant other plenty of room.

♥ Make sure you get plenty of space from him.

> To believe your own thought,
> to believe that what is true for
> you in your private heart is true
> for all men—that is genius.
>
> Ralph Waldo Emerson

Do you ever think about how many times a year the average married couple has sex?

♥ In the United States, the average married couple has sex 138 times per year.

♥ In Canada, the number increases to 150 times per year.

♥ In France (where love is always in the air) they have sex 167 times per year.

> Follow your bliss.
> James Campbell

279

Do you ever think about getting a tattoo?

♥ Many upper-class singles are turned off by tattoos.

280

What are your feelings regarding Dutch treat dating?

♥ Many women still believe that men should pay for most, if not all, of the dating expenses.

♥ Would you gain anything from paying your own way?

Do you believe in love at first sight?

♥ How can you love someone you don't know?

♥ Could love at first sight really be infatuation?

♥ Studies show that people who believe in love at first sight are more likely to experience it.

> Whenever you want to marry someone, go have lunch with his ex-wife.
>
> Shelly Winters

282

Would you consider marrying someone who has been married before?

♥ The odds are against second and third marriages working out.

♥ Sixty percent of all second marriages end in divorce.

♥ Seventy percent of all third marriages end in divorce.

> The trouble with marriage is that, while every woman is at heart a mother, every man is at heart a bachelor.
>
> E.V. Lucas

How much time do you spend watching television?

💜 The average person has their television on for four hours a day.

💜 How about spending that time developing a higher quality of social life?

It's loving and giving that make life worth living.

UNKNOWN

Are you superstitious?

💜 How does it affect your love life?

💜 Would you accept a first date offer on a Friday the 13?

💜 Do you have any good luck charms that you carry with you on dates?

> Youth is not a time of life—it is a state of mind.
> Samuel Ullman

285

Do you ever turn down a date because he asked you out at the last minute?

💜 More than 60 percent of women say that they have turned down dates who waited past Thursday afternoon to ask them out for a weekend date.

💜 Half of those women regret not going out on those missed dates.

> Women are meant to be loved, not to be understood.
>
> Oscar Wilde

286

Do you ever go after men who are unavailable?

♥ Are you afraid of love?

♥ Are you afraid of commitment?

287

How does your work ethic affect your love life?

♥ Does your significant other see you as a lazy bum or as a workaholic?

♥ Or do you have the right balance between work and love?

288

Do you look for the good in others?

♥ Many people who have been hurt by love keep their radar zooming in for character flaws, and once they find out that their love interest isn't perfect, they ditch him. The problem with this type of behavior is that no one is perfect, so they end up destroying some potentially great relationships.

> Love is not blind.
> It sees more, not less.
> But because it sees more, it
> is willing to see less.
>
> Rabbi Julius Gordon

289

How do you treat your pet in front of your significant other?

♥ Many people view pets as child substitutes. Does your love interest see you as a great mom for his future children or as a harsh taskmaster?

290

Do you ever think about how your significant other wants to please you?

♥ Compliment his efforts. Everyone wants and needs to feel appreciated!

Do you ever think about how you and your old flames might one day meet again in heaven?

Does that bring you comfort?

Does that make you regret how you treated some of the men in your past?

> Bachelor: a man who wouldn't take yes for an answer.
>
> Family Circle

What would your neighbors think of your love life?

💜 Are you living a respectable lifestyle?

💜 Keep in mind that people will gossip.

> The way to gain a good
> reputation is to endeavor to be
> what you desire to appear.
>
> Socrates

293

Do you ever think about your role in creating a happy marriage?

♥ Many people believe that happy marriages just happen. They don't. It takes hard work to make a marriage work.

> When a couple agree to try marriage and get a divorce if it doesn't work, it's just doing wrong with a license.
>
> Betty Alexander

294

Do you ever think about how wisdom comes with age?

💜 Learn from your past.

💜 Ask older women for advice.

💜 Ask married women for advice.

Knowledge is power.
Ethel Watts Mumford

Do you love or hate Valentine's Day?

♥ Valentine's Day is often one of the happiest holidays for women when they are involved in a serious relationship.

♥ Many women report that it is one of the worst days of the year when they aren't dating. New Year's Eve is the only other holiday that women report feeling such strong opinions over.

Do you ever think about how one day you will be old?

💜 How does that affect your love-life plans?

💜 Do you want to stay single longer to take advantage of these carefree days?

💜 Or do you wish that you had a mate and a family already?

> You need to claim the events of your life to make yourself yours. When you truly possess all you have been and done, which may take some time, you are fierce with reality.
>
> Florida Scott-Maxwell

297

Do you ever think about how someday your own children will be dating?

♥ What will you tell them about love?

♥ Will you be a good advisor, or will you be bitter?

♥ Are you living your beliefs?

♥ Will your kids be proud of your choices?

♥ Will your children have to suffer for your mistakes?

298

Do you ever think about how if you whisper when you feel like yelling, you will end up having fewer arguments?

♥ Lower your voice and you lower the number of disagreements that you have.

> Praise does wonders
> for your sense of hearing.
> Arnold H. Glascow

299

Do you ever force your dreams on your significant other?

♥ The only person you should try to change is yourself.

♥ You are only headed for trouble when you try to change others.

300

Do you believe that it is still a man's world?

♥ If you do, what changes can you make?

♥ Do you play second fiddle to men?

301

How does your significant other treat your pet?

💜 Is he kind?

💜 Is he patient?

💜 Does he have a nurturing side to him?

> In every negative event
> is the seed of an equal
> or greater benefit.
>
> Napoleon Hill

Do you ever think about how the majority of dog owners say that they are closer to their dogs than they are to their friends?

 Will he love you as much as he loves his dog?

 Do you love his dog?

We tell ourselves stories in order to live.

Joan Didion

303

What would you do if your significant other didn't like your best friend?

♥ Most women still continue their friendships.

304

Do you ever think about why women buy most of the self-help books?

♥ Studies show that psychology and self-improvement are two areas that women are generally much more interested in than their male counterparts.

305

Do you ever think about
how more than 60 percent
of women feel that they have
settled down after marriage?

The majority of those women didn't like feeling
this way.

Why do so many women rush to marry?

> There is no agony
> like bearing an untold
> story inside you.
> Zora Neale Hurston

306

Do you ever think about
the fact that 110 million
Americans own a pet?

♥ Odds are that you will marry an animal lover.

♥ How does that make you feel?

♥ Are you allergic to pets?

307

Do you ever wish you could have lunch with his ex-girlfriend?

♥ What would you really want to know?

♥ Is there something about him that worries you?

♥ Do you secretly compare yourself to her?

> You train people how to treat you by how you treat yourself.
>
> Martin Rutte

308

Do you jump to conclusions about your boyfriend's behavior and motives?

💜 Take your time and find out the truth.

💜 When in doubt, ask him.

309

Do you ever take phone calls when you are out on a date?

💜 Single men under twenty-five revealed that one of their biggest peeves was girlfriends who talked to their friends while out on a date.

💜 Turn off your cell phone!

Do you ever compete with your boyfriends?

❤ Are you a competitive person?

❤ If you compete with your female friends, you are twice as likely to compete with your boyfriend.

❤ Competition between a couple can ruin the best of relationships. Learn to stop the competition.

311

Do you ever think about the fact that more than 90 percent of men say their significant other is their best friend?

♥ Are you a true pal to your significant other?

> The secret to a happy marriage is simple: just keep on being as polite to one another as you are to your best friend.
>
> Robert Quillen

Do you ever think about the prayers your significant other prays about you?

 Is he asking God to change you?

Is he asking God to make this relationship last forever?

Is he thanking God for bringing you into his life?

313

Would you want to be friends with your significant other if he were a woman?

💜 Do you like him?

💜 Are you interested in the same things?

💜 Are you supportive of each other?

💜 Do you respect his opinions?

There is more here than meets the eye.

Lady Murasaki

255

314

What does your significant other think about your career?

 Is he proud of you?

 Does he support you?

 If you were to marry and have children, what would become of your career in his eyes?

 Does he show an active interest in your work?

We tend to get what we expect.

Norman Vincent Peale

315

What is your significant other like when he gets home from work?

💜 Is he grumpy?

💜 Is he tired?

💜 If he had a bad day, does he take it out on you?

💜 Does he share stories about his day with you?

💜 Do you know his coworkers?

316

If a television producer made a documentary about dating based on the last six months of your love life, would it be a drama, comedy, horror film, tearjerker, or the love story of the century?

💜 Are you happy with your answer? If not, try shaking things up a bit.

💜 What kind of story would you want it to be?

Do you mean what you say to potential dates?

💜 Do you simply try to impress men and be what you think they want you to be?

💜 Do you give insincere compliments?

💜 Do you resort to giving your same old lines?

💜 Be yourself!

> We awaken in others the same attitude of mind we hold toward them.
>
> Elbert Hubbard

318

Do you ever include your boyfriend in some of the activities you enjoy doing with your family?

💜 See what he is like around the people you love the most.

💜 Do they like him?

💜 Does he fit in with them?

💜 Are you proud of him? If not, move on quickly.

319

Is your significant other a spendthrift or a miser?

♥ Are you comfortable with his financial style?

320

Do you ever think about whether your parents were faithful to each other?

♥ If not, has that made you more determined to be faithful?

♥ If they weren't, have you learned from their mistakes?

321

Do you ever confuse love and infatuation?

♥ Look up the two definitions in the dictionary.

♥ If you confuse the two, maybe you are just trying to rush things. Take it slowly.

322

Do you ever think about what colors your home is decorated in?

♥ Many men report not feeling comfortable in overly feminine rooms.

Are you rude to your dates?

💜 Are you late?

💜 Do you spend too much of their money when you go out?

💜 Do you flirt with other men?

💜 Ask your friends for their opinions.

> The word intimacy comes from a Latin root that means innermost.
>
> Susan Wittig Albert

Do you ever think about being faithful to the same man for the rest of your life?

💜 How does that make you feel?

💜 If you aren't ready to make such a huge commitment, don't rush into marriage. Wait until you are ready.

All things are difficult before they are easy.

Thomas Fuller

325

Do you ever think about what you want out of your entire life and not just your love life?

💜 Write it out.

💜 Be specific.

💜 Make a detailed plan for the next fifty years.

> You can have anything you want if you want it desperately enough. You must want it with an inner exuberance that erupts through the skin and joins the energy that created the world.
>
> Sheilah Graham

326

Do you ever think about what your significant other will get you for Christmas?

♥ Thirty-five percent of all Christmas gifts are bought the week before Christmas.

♥ Seventy-one percent of last-minute Christmas Eve shoppers are men.

If you don't ask, you don't get.
Mohandas K. Gandhi

266

Has your past made you suspicious of men?

♥ Trust is one of the most important ingredients in a relationship.

♥ Try trusting until your trust isn't warranted. If he breaks your trust, give him the boot.

♥ Be sure that you can always trust yourself.

> One way or another, women have been telling each other, "If you want to get married, don't ask questions."
>
> Mary Kay Blakely

Do you ever think about how men say they notice a woman's smile within the first twenty seconds of meeting her?

♥ Try to smile a lot to show the world that you are an open, warm person.

♥ Do all that you can to have an inviting smile.

329

Do you ever think
about the meaning behind
your sarcastic comments
regarding your love life?

♥ What do your jokes really mean?

♥ Are you hiding your pain?

> When in doubt,
> Mumble.
>
> James H. Boren

330

Do you ever think about your dream home?

♥ The cost for the median home in the United States is now $159,600.

♥ What style of home do you love?

♥ Is it in the country or the city?

♥ Is it large or small?

270

Do you ever compare yourself to your significant other's old girlfriends?

💜 Keep in mind that they are history. You are the woman in his life.

💜 Forget the old girlfriends.

> Often people attempt to live their lives backwards; they try to have more things, or money, in order to do more of what they want so that they will be happier. The way it actually works is the reverse. You must first be who you really are and then do what you need to do, in order to have what you want.
>
> Margaret Young

332

How does your significant other act around children?

♥ Does he have the potential to be a great dad?

♥ Is he clueless around kids?

♥ Try to baby-sit with him and see what he is really like.

333

Do you ever think about buying fewer clothes but more expensive ones?

♥ Remember that clothes can make a woman feel great. When you feel good, you look good.

334

Who are your significant other's role models?

💜 Ask yourself what your feelings are regarding these people.

💜 Ask yourself if he values the qualities in others that you value.

💜 Does he even have any role models?

335

Do you ever visit with your significant other's mom?

♥ You can learn a ton from her!

♥ Remember the old advice that men who are good to their mothers are good to their wives.

♥ Would you like this woman as your mother-in-law?

> With every rising of
> the sun, think of your
> life as just begun.
>
> UNKNOWN

336

Do you ever think about how your energy level affects your love life?

♥ Get plenty of rest.

♥ Exercise.

♥ Take your vitamins.

We find rest in those
we love, and we provide
a resting place in ourselves
for those who love us.

St. Bernard of Clairvaux

When you were young,
did you dream of a life of
adventure on your own or
of a life of romance with
the man of your dreams?

Revisit those old dreams, for you might find
your true calling there.

The entire sum of existence
is the magic of being needed
by just one person.

Vi Putnam

Do you ever think that if you haven't learned your lessons from your past dating mistakes, then you will probably repeat those mistakes until you do?

💜 Try to learn from your love life blunders and move on from there.

💜 What mistakes do you keep repeating?

The more failures, the more success. Period.

Tom Peters

339

Do you keep a clothes diary to keep track of the outfits you wear on each date?

♥ You can also keep track of how much money you spend on your dating wardrobe. You might just be shocked by the amount!

When in doubt, wear red.

Bill Blass

Do you ever think about how people form their first impressions?

💜 First impressions are important.

💜 It is hard to change someone's mind once he has formed a first impression of you.

💜 Here is the order in which people make their first judgments regarding another person:

   1. Gender
   2. Race
   3. Body type
   4. Facial expression

341

Are you friends with your significant other's sisters?

♥ You can learn a great deal about your love interest that way.

♥ You can also decide if you would fit in with his family.

342

What would you would do if you fell in love with someone but didn't like his family?

♥ In-law problems can wreak havoc on couples.

♥ If you don't like his family, only proceed with a great deal of consideration.

343

What signals is your significant other sending you?

💜 Listen to his words, but pay extremely close attention to his actions.

💜 Remember the old adage about actions speaking louder than words.

> A man is known by
> the company he keeps.
> English Proverb

344

Is your career or your love life near the top of your list of priorities?

♥ Only 15.7 percent of the top executives at America's largest companies are women.

♥ It can be quite difficult for many women to juggle a career, husband, children, and aging parents all at the same time.

> You must learn day by day, year by year, to broaden your horizon. The more things you love, the more you are interested in, the more you enjoy, the more you are indignant about—the more you have left when anything happens.
>
> Ethel Barrymore

345

What song would represent your last romantic relationship?

♥ Go back and give each of your serious love affairs a theme song to bring a sense of closure and understanding to them.

> A happy marriage is a long conversation that always seems too short.
>
> Andre Maurois

Do you ever think about how men and women's expectations may change after marriage regarding their partner's behavior?

Studies show that both sexes expect their partners to act more mature after the wedding.

> Marriages are made in heaven, but they are lived on earth.
> Nathan Howard Gist

What does your home reveal to your boyfriends?

♥ It shows your taste.

♥ It may reveal some of your hobbies.

♥ It shows your level of tidiness.

♥ It reveals where you are comfortable living.

♥ It shows off personal memorabilia, such as photographs and decorative treasures.

348

Do you ever use affirmations to improve your love life?

♥ They can be quite helpful in gaining a new social skill or increasing your self-esteem.

♥ Write out some positive affirmations regarding your self-esteem and your love life. Read them in the morning and at bedtime.

349

What does your vehicle reveal about you to a future mate?

♥ It shows off your neatness level.

♥ If you buy into the theory that you are what you drive, then you really are making a statement with your choice of cars.

350

Do you ever think about how married people live longer than their single counterparts?

♥ That should inspire even the most steadfast of bachelors to consider eventually getting married.

351

Do you ever attend an event outside of your comfort zone or areas of interest in order to meet some new singles?

♥ Try it. You might meet some great new people.

♥ If you feel a bit nervous about it, bring a buddy along.

♥ Who knows, you might just find a new hobby that you love along with Mr. Right.

Action conquers fear.
Peter Nivio Zarlenga

Do you have enough friends outside of your career and work arena?

♥ It could be that you need to concentrate more on your social life away from your job in order to improve your love life.

♥ Making some new friends can give you a whole new outlook on life.

> A tough lesson in life that one has to learn is that not everybody wishes you well.
>
> Dan Rather

353

What "rules" do you have for your love life?

♥ Everyone needs a set of guidelines to follow in their heart and head so that they know how to act in all dating situations.

♥ Just make sure that your rules are the ones that work for you.

♥ Keep your rules honest and ethical. Never play games.

354

What do you pray for regarding your love life?

💜 What do you really want?

💜 Do you have faith that your prayers will be answered?

💜 Ask your family and friends to pray for you.

> The story of a love is not important. What is important is that one is capable of love.
>
> Helen Hayes

355

How are your cooking skills?

♥ The majority of men say that they would like to marry a woman who is a great cook.

♥ Consider taking a cooking class. You will learn how to be a better cook, plus you might meet Mr. Right. The number of men in gourmet cooking classes has increased 27 percent over the last ten years.

What is "true" for you regarding love?

♥ What is your philosophy?

♥ Do you really know what you believe in your heart of hearts?

♥ What do you expect to happen?

> Worry a little bit every day, and in a lifetime you will lose a couple of years. If something is wrong, fix it if you can. But train yourself not to worry. Worry never fixes anything.
>
> Mary Hemingway

357

Do you ever think about how younger Americans are likely to divorce?

♥ Forty-two percent of those who get divorced are in the 25 to 34 age bracket.

358

Do the little things that you buy reveal your romantic side?

♥ Music, candles, gourmet foods, wine, and fine chocolates can all add a bit of romance to your life even if you haven't had a date in months.

Do you ever take yourself out for a great Saturday night date?

💜 There is no reason to sit at home just because you don't have a man in your life.

💜 Get out there and kick up your heels.

💜 Treat yourself to a great meal.

💜 Dress up.

💜 If you don't want to go it alone, invite some friends to join you.

360

Do you ever think about throwing yourself a huge pity party after a really bad date or a breakup?

♥ Invite your best girlfriends over for male bashing.

♥ Have some good laughs at your own expense and cheer yourself up.

> Your closest relationships seem to matter most for your health.
>
> Dr. Janice Kiecolt-Glaser

361

Do you give your date your full attention?

♥ Do you spend much of your time worried over your own behavior?

♥ Are you busy watching other people?

> Difficult times have helped me to understand better than before how infinitely rich and beautiful life is in every way and that so many things that one goes worrying about are of no importance whatsoever.
>
> Isak Dinesen

362

Do you ever think about
how you can improve your
love life through reading
great literature?

❤ You can become inspired by the characters.

❤ You can join a book club and meet some new
friends.

❤ You can discuss your book selection on your
next date.

Do you ever set goals to improve your social life?

💜 Set up a plan to call a different friend for lunch each week.

💜 Invite a group of acquaintances over for dinner.

💜 Get to know a different neighbor each month.

💜 Plan to throw a block party with your neighbors.

💜 Organize a singles' group at your church.

💜 Get your friends to matchmake for you once a month.

Do you ever think about making a scrapbook of all your old flames?

💜 Is there a pattern to how these relationships ended?

💜 Do you always date the same type of man?

💜 What do you think of these former beaus now?

> Some women wait for something to change and nothing does change so they change themselves.
> Audre Lorde

365

Do you ever think about doing
some little holiday gestures
to show the man in your
life that you care?

♥ Try:

1. buying candy for Valentine's Day,

2. putting his name on an Easter egg,

3. inviting him on a Memorial Day picnic,

4. buying some fireworks to shoot off
   together on the Fourth of July,

5. going trick-or-treating together,

6. inviting him over for Thanksgiving dinner,

7. decorating his place at Christmas.

366

Do you ever think about making a graph to see how you spend your weekends?

♥ Time can be squandered so easily. It is a good thing to know if you can spend your time more wisely.

367

Do you ever think about how your self-image will change once you become a wife?

♥ What do you think that will mean to you?

Do you ever rate your dates?

💜 Keep track of how much you enjoyed the man's company.

💜 Write down your gut feeling regarding your compatibility.

💜 Make just a few notes about the overall quality of the date.

💜 You might be surprised about your feelings once you see them written out right before your eyes. "Mr. Right" may not be quite so wonderful once you see him in black and white.

How would you would feel
if you and your significant
other were trapped in
a cave for a week?

♥ Would he be your knight in shining armor, or
would you have to take care of him?

♥ What was your initial reaction to the idea of being
stranded alone with him?

Light is the
symbol of truth.
James Russell Lowell

370

Do you ever think about the fact that five million couples seek counseling with a family therapist each year?

Marriage isn't always easy!

> Love: a temporary insanity curable by marriage.
>
> Ambrose Bierce

371

How do your decision-making abilities affect your love life?

💜 Can you make good choices under pressure?

💜 Do you make up your mind easily?

💜 Do you listen to your intuition?

💜 Are you ruled by your head or heart?

💜 Are you interested in the entire picture?

> Associate yourself with
> men of good quality if you esteem
> your own reputation, for 'tis better
> to be alone than in bad company.
>
> George Washington

372

Do you ever think about how your self-image will change once you become a mother?

♥ How do you view women who are mothers? Do you still view them as sexy and vibrant?

373

Do you and your significant other have nicknames for each other?

♥ What is the meaning behind them?

♥ Are they kind and flattering?

Do you and your significant other ever wear matching clothes?

💜 Sixty-eight percent of couples say that they have dressed alike or in similar costumes for Halloween.

💜 Twenty-one percent of couples say that they have worn matching sweaters or shirts on at least one occasion.

Love is a canvas furnished by Nature and embroidered by imagination.

voltaire

375

What does his favorite charity reveal about your significant other's character?

💜 Does he love kids?

💜 Is he good with older people?

💜 Does he like helping the underdog?

Always do right—
this will gratify some
and astonish the rest.

Mark Twain

Do you ever think about getting more sleep?

♥ Research shows that most women could use at least one more hour of sleep per night.

♥ Americans are getting 20 percent less sleep now than they did in 1900.

♥ You think better and look better when you are well rested.

> We read books to find out who we are. What other people, real or imaginary, do and think and feel is an essential guide to our understanding of what we ourselves are and may become.
>
> Ursula K. LeGuin

377

Do you ever think about attending a love-life seminar?

♥ You may learn some helpful hints.

♥ You might meet Mr. Right.

378

Do you ever think about setting aside more time for solitude?

♥ You can learn about yourself.

♥ You can become more comfortable with being alone.

Do you ever think about joining a singles' group at your church?

💜 What have you got to lose by joining?

💜 Even if you don't meet Mr. Right, you might meet some great new female friends.

💜 Plus, you will realize that there are plenty of other singles out there looking for love just like you.

💜 Church groups can be a great support.

> Oh what use is love if you have no one to love?
>
> Immanuel of Rome

380

Did you know that getting married is one of the top priorities for 68 percent of singles?

💜 Remember that you aren't alone when you are looking for love. Millions of people are going through the same thing as you.

💜 Take comfort in knowing that you are not the only person wanting to get married.

> Your diamonds are not in far distant mountains or in yonder seas; they are in your own backyard, if you but dig for them.
>
> Russell H. Conwell

Do you help your friends whose love lives aren't nearly as happy and successful as yours?

💜 Talk to your single friends and offer your support.

💜 Matchmake whenever you can.

💜 Entertain those who never have dates and are going through a really dry spell.

> Never underestimate the value of luck, but remember that luck comes to those searching for something.
>
> Stanley Marcus

382

Do you ever think about how the majority of married women feel that they are the emotional caretakers in their marriages?

♥ Either plan on taking charge of the emotional issues or be sure to find a partner who is willing and able to share this important role. Otherwise you may resent your partner.

Love is a fruit in season at all times.

Mother Teresa

383

Do you ever think about how more than 85 percent of romance novels are purchased by women?

♥ We are a romantic bunch, aren't we?

384

What is your significant other's driving style?

♥ Would you want your children to ride with him?

♥ Is he courteous to other drivers?

♥ Do you like riding with him? Do you feel safe?

385

Do you overestimate or underestimate your desirability factor?

♥ Try to be realistic when you look at yourself.

♥ Ask a trusted friend for her input.

> Some of my best friends are illusions. Been sustaining me for years.
> Sheila Ballantyne

What color best describes your personality?

♥ Yellow = a sunny disposition.

♥ Blue = a calm demeanor.

♥ Pink = a feminine personality.

♥ Red = a fiery temperament.

♥ Green = a jealous side to the personality.

♥ Purple = a regal side to the personality.

Do you ever think about how unromantic marriage can seem at times?

Mortgages, taxes, child-care issues, utility bills, car payments, aging parents, and medical problems can be draining to even the most romantic of couples.

Though we travel the world over to find the beautiful, we must carry it with us or we find it not.

Ralph Waldo Emerson

388

What do your eating habits say about you?

♥ Do others see you as an expert on gourmet cooking?

♥ Do you eat only healthy foods and look like a health-conscious soul?

♥ Do you always eat on the run?

♥ Are you the queen of junk food?

We are the heroes of our own story.
Mary McCarthy

389

Do you ever think about
how a hundred years ago
marriages only lasted fifteen
to twenty years and then
the people died?

💜 Nowadays marriages can last for fifty or more years.

💜 "Til death do us part" can seem like forever if you are married to the wrong person.

389

Do you ever think about
how many men say
that they will call after
a date and then don't?

Don't always believe a date when he says he will
call you. If you haven't heard from him and you
still want to, call him. What do you have to lose?

To love oneself
is the beginning of
a lifelong romance.

Oscar Wilde

Do you ever think about the real value of female friendships?

💜 Female friends validate your feelings.

💜 They are there to see you through good times and bad.

💜 You can share your love-life woes.

💜 You can share fun activities together.

💜 Never underestimate the power of friendships.

392

Do you ever try to hide parts of yourself from others?

♥ Do you hide more physical parts of yourself or emotional parts?

We live in an atmosphere of shame. We are ashamed of everything that is real about us: ashamed of ourselves, of our relatives, of our incomes, of our accents, of our opinions, of our experiences, just as we are ashamed of our naked skins.

George Bernard Shaw

393

Do you ever think about your parents' dating style?

💜 Learn from their failures.

💜 Take the good things that they did and copy what worked if it fits your style.

💜 Keep in mind that you are your own person and you don't have to follow in their footsteps.

Truth is in ourselves,
it takes no rise from outward
things, what'ere you may believe.

Robert Browning

Do you ever think about getting dating advice from your brother?

💜 Your brother can give you the lowdown on the male perspective.

💜 He can open your eyes to the male point of view.

> If you listen, you will double your charisma.
>
> David Niven

395

Do you ever think
about the quality of your
friends' love lives?

💜 Is yours like theirs?

💜 Are you living your own love life or just going
along with the pack?

> For everything there is
> an appointed time, even a time
> for every affair under heaven.
>
> Ecclesiastes 3:1

396

Do you ever think about the quality of your siblings' love lives?

💜 Are they successful in the romantic arena?

💜 Can you learn from watching their failures and successes?

💜 Are you proud of their dating behavior?

💜 Do all of you act alike when it comes to romance?

Give what thou hast, then shalt thou receive.

UNKNOWN

397

Are your romantic timelines realistic?

♥ The most successful marriage partners date for at least fifteen months before getting married.

398

Do you ever think about your biological clock?

♥ Do you feel pressured by it?

♥ Have you talked to your gynecologist regarding your concerns about your age? Get all of your questions answered.

399

Do you visualize success or failure for yourself?

Beware of self-fulfilling negative prophecies!

400

Do you ever think about writing out your own relationship contract?

Promise yourself that you won't date any men with addictions, low moral standards, abusive behaviors, or wives!

401

How are you influenced by your significant other?

♥ A good mate will make you want to be a better person.

402

What is your significant other like when he is sick?

♥ The average person catches nine colds a year.

♥ Be cautious of marrying a man who turns into a baby when he gets sick.

403

What cities do you think are most romantic?

💜 Call your travel agent and plan a dream vacation for yourself to one of them.

404

Do you like to hug and kiss?

💜 Many men aren't as comfortable with giving just hugs and kisses as women are.

💜 Are you a physically demonstrative person? If you are, then you will probably be happiest marrying someone who is much like yourself.

405

Do you have good manners?

♥ Both sexes agree that a mate with good social skills is important.

> Politeness in an individual
> is as necessary as paint on both
> sides of a fence, for a person, like
> a fence, faces out as well as in.
>
> Marcelene Cox

406

Do you ever attend religious services on your dates?

💜 Couples who have a strong spiritual foundation are less likely to divorce.

407

Do you ever think about the time of day that you want to get married?

💜 More than seventy percent of weddings take place during the day.

408

Do you ever think about what your wedding gown will look like?

 Will it be a family heirloom?

 What color will you choose?

 Who is your favorite designer?

 Who will you invite to shop with you when you go to pick it out?

 How much do you plan to spend on it?

> Undoubtedly, we become what we envision.
> Claude M. Bristol

409

Do you make financial
investments on your own,
or are you waiting until
you get married?

Never put off your financial planning, for if you
do, you are just cheating yourself out of financial
gains.

Take care of yourself financially.

Do it (what needs to
be done) for yourself as if
you were a dear friend.

Jerry Downs

410

Do you ever think about the Ten Commandments?

♥ Do you follow them in your love life?

411

Under what circumstances would you consider ending a marriage?

♥ Adultery and physical abuse are the main reasons that the majority of singles say they would leave a marriage.

412

Are you the one who usually ends your romantic relationships?

💜 Are you afraid of commitment?

💜 Are you always choosing the wrong kind of men?

💜 Do you bail out when you think that you will get dumped?

Love knows not its own depth until the hour of separation.
Kahlil Gibran

Do you ever think about the fact that if your current romantic relationship hasn't ever been truly fulfilling, it probably will never be?

💜 Learn to recognize a doomed love affair and move on.

💜 You are wasting precious time by holding on to false hope.

> It always comes back to the same thing: go deep enough and there is a bedrock of truth.
>
> May Sarton

414

Do you ever think about how you always have yourself to answer to?

♥ Learn to understand yourself so that you will be able to make your dreams come true.

415

Do you ever think about moving to Alaska to meet a man?

♥ Alaska has the best ratio of single men to single women of any state in the union.

Do you ever think about your significant other's high school days?

♥ Would you have liked him?

♥ Would you have belonged to the same social circles?

Sometimes a person has to go back, really back—to have a sense, an understanding of all that's gone to make them—before they can go forward.

Paul Marshall

417

Do you ever think about buying a home with a beautiful view?

♥ If you do, you will create a sense of romance for yourself.

♥ Consider one with a lovely fireplace, too.

> In my life's chain of events nothing was accidental. Everything happened according to an inner need.
>
> Hannah Senesh

418

How many children do you hope to have someday?

♥ The number of children per family has been dropping over the last few decades.

♥ The average number of children per family has now dropped to less than two per couple.

419

How is your opinion of a prospective date influenced by his profession?

♥ Do you limit yourself too much by only dating men who are on a certain career track?

420

Do you ever think about renting a limo to pick up your significant other for a special night out on the town?

♥ Little touches of romance can add sparkle to a big night.

♥ An element of surprise can add a bit of pizzazz to a date.

> It is always better to be an original than an imitation.
>
> Theodore Roosevelt

421

Do you ever think about volunteering to baby-sit for your married friends and asking them to pay you in set-ups with their single friends?

💜 Many couples meet through blind dates.

💜 Your married friends will appreciate your kindness to their love life.

Do you ever think about
how more women live longer
after a husband dies than
men do after a wife dies?

♥ Women are tough and courageous.

♥ We can handle life without men much better
than we let on.

> If we all did the things we
> are capable of doing, we would
> literally astound ourselves.
>
> Thomas Edison

Do you ever give romantic gifts?

♥ Add a touch of romance whenever you can.

♥ Wrap your presents beautifully to make them even more special.

Love is
sentimental measles.
Charles Kingsley

How do you feel regarding a potential mate's income?

💜 Do you prefer to date men who earn more than you earn? Many women go down this path. The problem is that if you limit your dating pool based on income, you can seriously hurt your chances of finding a mate.

💜 The fewer restrictions you have on your dating pool, the more men you will be able to date. However, everyone needs to have their own standards and to feel comfortable with their choices.

Don't marry for money.
You can borrow it cheaper.

Scottish proverb

425

Do you ever think about the great love scenes that you have watched in the movies?

Rent a love story for the next time you wish you had and date and don't. You can live vicariously through the lovers in the film.

426

Do you ever think about double dating with your parents?

I don't recommend this for first dates, but once you become a couple, you might enjoy going out socially with your folks from time to time.

427

Do you have a courageous heart when it comes to love?

♥ Finding true love can require you to be strong and brave.

428

Do you ever think about how independent you are?

♥ Many independent singles have a little trouble making a commitment.

429

Do you ever think about walking during some of your dates instead of driving?

♥ Conversations can really become intimate during a leisurely stroll.

♥ Walking is great exercise and gets the endorphin levels up in your body, which can make you feel even happier.

> The first of earthly blessings, independence.
>
> Edward Gibbon

Do you ever think about going to a singles' resort on your next vacation?

💜 Take a friend along if you feel uncomfortable going it alone.

> People waste more time waiting for someone to take charge of their lives than they do in any other pursuit. Time is life. Time is all there is.
>
> Gloria Steinem

431

Do you ever think about hiring a decorator to fix up your home?

♥ It is important to present a flattering picture of yourself and your lifestyle to prospective mates.

432

Do you ever think about the Bible's definition of love?

♥ Read 1 Corinthians.

♥ Talk to your minister about real love.

433

Do you ever think about taking dance lessons?

♥ Dancing is so romantic.

♥ Dancing is much more enjoyable when you are a good dancer.

♥ You might meet an interesting man at the dance studio.

♥ Many dance studios host dance parties for singles and couples.

Do you ever think about sending yourself a fabulous Valentine's Day gift when you aren't seeing anyone special on February 14?

♥ Treat yourself. You deserve it!

Let us not be particular; it is better to have old secondhand diamonds than none at all.

Mark Twain

435

Do you ever think about the way you decorate for the holidays?

♥ Celebrate. Decorate. Use any excuse to make the day more special.

♥ Never put off decorating until you have a mate. Many singles miss out on lots of holiday fun because they refuse to decorate their homes if they live alone.

> Love is the triumph of imagination over intelligence.
> H.L. Mencken

436

Do you have just a few activities that you do on dates and do you keep repeating them over and over again?

♥ Try new things to keep your dates exciting.

♥ The most popular dates that get repeated again and again are:

Movies
Dinner dates
Parties
Sporting events
Concerts

Do you ever think about fixing a romantic picnic for your next date?

♥ Try a variation of an old favorite if you don't like just a good old-fashioned picnic. Consider:

A moonlight picnic

A rooftop picnic

A living-room picnic by candlelight

A gourmet picnic

A picnic in the snow complete with hot chocolate and s'mores

A campfire picnic

A beach picnic

A mountaintop picnic

438

Do you ever think about throwing a party for you and your best friends at a romantic bed and breakfast?

💜 Enjoy special spots without a man.

💜 Get out of your normal routine.

💜 LIVE IT UP!

variety is the spice of life.

UNKNOWN

439

Do you ever think about buying yourself a fabulous gift to celebrate being single?

♥ Why not? Consider:

A new car

A beautiful strand of pearls

A membership to a club that you have always wanted to join

A pair of diamond earrings

A lovely piece of 18 karat gold jewelry

A new wardrobe

Do you ever think about how you treat yourself?

💜 You need to be your own best friend.

💜 If you don't take good care of yourself and respect yourself, how can you expect others to do so?

> I read and walked for miles at night along the beach, writing bad blank verse and searching endlessly for someone wonderful who would step out of the darkness and change my life. It never crossed my mind that that person could be me.
>
> Anna Quindlen

441

Do you ever think about which flowers are the most romantic?

The most popular flowers of romance are:

Roses

Forget-Me-Nots

Tulips

Gardenias

Orchids

Unfulfilled desires
are dangerous forces.
Sarah Tableton Calvin

442

Do you believe that the best days of your life are behind you or in front of you?

♥ To be truly happy, you must believe that they are in the present.

443

Do you like yourself as much after a date as you did before the date?

♥ Remain true to yourself and your values and you will always like yourself as well after dates.

Do you ever think about what age of men you are most attracted to?

💙 Do you date that age group?

💙 Are you looking for a father figure?

💙 Are you only comfortable with your peer group?

💙 Do you date younger men because you feel more comfortable with them?

💙 The more age groups that you open yourself up to, the more men you have to choose from. Just remember that large variations in a couple's ages can often produce difficulties that need to be addressed.

Are you sacrificing your health in order to be attractive to members of the opposite sex?

💜 Tanning too much can cause skin cancer.

💜 Many women try to be too thin, which isn't healthy.

💜 Drinking too much alcohol isn't healthy either.

> We are always afraid to start something that we want to make very good, true, and serious.
>
> Brenda Ueland

How do you know when you are in love?

♥ Most people say that they know it when they feel a sense of profound belonging, a sense of excitement, a physical attraction that is very strong, and a sense of being understood at a very deep level.

> Love...binds everything together in perfect harmony.
>
> Colossians 8:14

447

How do you behave at parties?

♥ Are you a wallflower, the life of the party, or somewhere in between?

♥ Come up with some good conversation starters before you go to a party to help you mingle better.

♥ Force yourself to mingle with members of the opposite sex.

♥ Ask your friends to introduce you to any men that you find attractive if you don't want to approach them on your own.

♥ Smile and practice having relaxed body language.

448

Do you ever think about what the great poets have written about love?

Try reading Robert Browning, Elizabeth Barrett Browning, Shakespeare, or Keats.

449

How long does it take you to decide if you want to date someone?

What factors come into play for you?

450

Do you ever think about how problems with one's in-laws contribute to two out of three divorces in this country?

♥ Look closely at his family before saying yes.

> In England there is a law prohibiting a man from marrying his mother-in-law. A law like that is not needed in the United States.
>
> UNKNOWN

Do you ever get a headache when you are out on a date?

♥ Your body may be trying to tell you that you are out with the wrong man or that you are worrying too much.

♥ Learn to recognize headaches that are brought on by stress-related events.

> If you want to find the answers to the big questions about your soul, you'd best begin with the little answers about your body.
>
> Dr. George Sheehan

Did you know that more weddings take place in California than any other state?

♥ Obviously the state has a large population, but it is also has lovely scenery.

Perhaps loving something is
the only starting place there is
for making your life your own.

Alice Koller

453

Did you know that January is the least popular month of the year for weddings?

♥ The weather is the number-one reason people shy away from planning a January wedding.

> Success in marriage is much more than finding the right person; it is a matter of being the right person.
>
> B.R. Brickner

Do you ever think about
what you would want
your bridesmaids to wear
at your wedding?

♥ More than 83 percent of bridesmaids never
wear those dresses again.

> What a gift of grace
> to be able to take the chaos
> from within and from it create
> some semblance of order.
>
> Katherine Paterson

455

Do you ever think about whether you secretly enjoy the heartaches in your friends' love lives?

♥ Misery loves company.

456

Do you ever think about what you believe Mr. Right will bring to your life?

♥ Give that to yourself. Don't wait for him to do it!

Do you ever think about how only a tiny minority of women propose to their significant other?

💜 Would you ever feel comfortable popping the big question?

💜 What would it take to make you want to ask him to marry you?

> To love and win is the best thing; to love and lose the next best.
>
> William Makepeace Thackeray

Do you ever think about whether your parents were physically expressive with each other in front of you?

♥ Most adults copy the behavior of their parents when it comes to marital behavior.

♥ Observe closely how your significant other's parents relate to each other.

To know oneself, one should assert oneself.

Albert Camus

459

Do you ever try to avoid suffering from a broken heart and therefore keep yourself from falling madly in love?

💜 Stop playing it too safe.

💜 Dare to fall in love.

💜 Remember the old adage of nothing ventured, nothing gained.

> Love consists in this, that two solitudes protect and touch and greet each other.
>
> Rainer Maria Rilke

460

Do you ever think about how the roles of men and women are changing over time?

♥ Look forward.

♥ Make sure your expectations are realistic when it comes to the roles we all play.

> The truth that many people never understand until it is too late is that the more you try to avoid suffering the more you suffer because smaller and more insignificant things begin to torture you in proportion to your fear of being hurt.
>
> Thomas Merton

Do you believe that you can't be happy on your own?

♥ Remember, the latest research proves that the happiest group of people in our society is single women.

♥ Take advantage of this special time on your own.

♥ There are more than eighty million single adults in the United States.

> Leisure requires the evidence of our own feelings, because it is not so much a quality of time as a peculiar state of mind.
>
> Vernon Lee

462

What things do you think of as being truly romantic?

💙 Make a list and add these elements to your world.

💙 The following is a list of things that are the most popular choices in the romance department:

> Moonlight
> Starry nights
> Candles
> Soft music
> Poetry
> Fine wine
> Romantic restaurants
> Fireplaces

463

Do you ever browse in a bookstore to meet a new man?

💜 Bookstores are now one of the top ten places for singles to meet.

464

What is your body language saying?

💜 An open, relaxed posture can make you seem friendly and inviting.

💜 Easy movements can give you an appearance of grace and self-confidence.

465

Do you ever think about taking a keen interest in an activity or hobby that appeals mostly to the opposite sex?

♥ You just might meet Mr. Right along the way.

> Keep changing. When you're
> through changing, you're through.
> Bruce Barton

466

Do you ever think about becoming a foster parent or adopting a child even though you are single?

💜 There are more than five hundred thousand children in United States who are in the foster-care system and more than one hundred thousand of those kids are waiting to be adopted.

💜 Many foreign countries allow single people to adopt, including Russia, China, and Guatemala.

💜 Each year, more and more singles are choosing to adopt.

467

Do you ever just blow off holidays when you aren't dating?

♥ If you do, then you are wasting possibly some of the best days of your life.

468

Do you ever think about taking a dream vacation after a traumatic break-up?

♥ Most people stay home and feel worse.

♥ A fabulous trip can help you to forget your heartache.

469

Do you ever think about working with a wardrobe consultant?

Most major department stores offer personal shopping services free of charge, and you might improve your appearance by working with a professional who can update your look.

> Well-ordered self-love is right and natural.
>
> Thomas Aquinas

470

Are you good at meeting attractive strangers?

♥ Don't let shyness stop you.

♥ Make it a game to meet at least one new single guy a week.

> The way you overcome shyness is to become so wrapped up in something you forget to be afraid.
>
> Lady Bird Johnson

Are you good at remembering people's names?

💜 This is a good trait to develop.

💜 People hate it when you forget their names or get their names wrong.

💜 People also love to hear their own names used in conversation.

> If you have charm, you don't need anything else. And if you don't have it, it doesn't matter what else you have.
>
> Sir James Barrie

472

Do you ever think about asking an "old maid" for dating advice?

♥ You might get advice that you never expected to hear!

473

Do you ever think about sending yourself flowers?

♥ Make it a beautiful bouquet of your favorites.

♥ Treat yourself the way you want Mr. Right to treat you.

Do you ever think about tucking yourself into bed after a really bad date with cocoa, animal crackers, and your old teddy bear?

♥ It can help you to feel all safe and loved again.

Ah, the relationships we get into just to get out of the ones we are not brave enough to say are over.

Julia Phillips

How often do you do activities that you love to do?

♥ So often we are too busy going through life to enjoy it.

♥ Schedule time for yourself to do the things you love to do.

> Don't put off for tomorrow what you can do today, because if you enjoy it today you can do it again tomorrow.
>
> James Michener

476

Do you ever think about double dating with your siblings?

 There is strength in numbers.

 You can get their opinion on the man in your life.

 You can enjoy your siblings as friends.

477

Do you ever think about starting a romantic book club?

💜 Check with your local bookstores about holding meetings there. Many stores are more than happy to have prospective book buyers meet at their stores.

478

Do you ever think about traveling to Paris in the springtime?

💜 You aren't getting any younger, so why wait?

Do you ever think about taking a singles' cruise on your next vacation?

♥ Grab a single gal pal and head off on a grand adventure.

> I am one of those who never knows the direction of my journey until I have arrived.
>
> Anna Louise Strong

Do you ever think about getting a part-time job to meet eligible men?

♥ Some part-time jobs that would allow you to meet men of all backgrounds and wouldn't take up too much of your time are:

Salesperson at a men's clothing store

Clerk at a bookstore

Bartender

Receptionist at a health club

Salesperson at an electronics store

Clerk at a sporting goods store

Volunteer at an animal shelter

Volunteer at your local library

481

Do you ever think about the things your grandparents did on dates?

♥ Incorporate some of this old-fashioned fun into your dating plans.

♥ Mix things up with some "blasts from the past."

482

Do you ever think about those old days when couples had chaperones along on dates?

♥ It makes three really seem like a crowd, doesn't it?

483

Do you ever think about trying to meet a new beau at your class reunion?

💜 It could be that you will fall in love with someone you never knew in school.

💜 A man could have changed a ton since the old days.

💜 The timing might be just right for you and an old classmate.

I've always thought that you have to believe in luck to get it.

Victoria Holt

484

Do you ever think about
what it will be like to attend
your significant other's
family reunion?

♥ Look closely at all of his relatives.

♥ Ask yourself if you want these people as your
family.

♥ Would you want your children to take after these
people?

♥ Check to see how you feel in their company.

485

What season do you find most romantic?

💜 Most singles prefer springtime.

486

Do you ever think about joining a religious sect that doesn't allow marriage?

💜 If you have, consider taking a sabbatical from the dating world.

When was the last time you made a new friend?

 Work hard at always making new friends.

 Your social life will then remain vital.

 You can never have too many buddies.

 You can never tell when a friend might introduce you to Mr. Right.

> Know thine opportunity.
>
> Pittacus

488

Do you ever think about appearing on a reality-based television show?

♥ Thousands of women have tried to get on The Bachelor.

♥ Thousands of women were offended by it.

> Just trust yourself, then you will know how to live.
>
> Johann Wolfgang von Goethe

What criteria do you use to judge a potential mate?

Most singles admit to using the following criteria:

Appearance

Personality

Social status

Direct your eye right inward, and you'll find a thousand regions in your mind yet undiscovered. Travel them and be expert in home cosmography.

Henry David Thoreau

490

Would you treat a man who is a plumber the same as you would a man who is an investment banker?

 Only you know in your heart if you believe that all men are created equal.

> Nobody knows what I am trying to do, but I do, and I know when I succeed.
>
> Gertrude Stein

491

Do you ever think about whether you will make a good parent?

 A good indication of your potential is how much you truly enjoy being around little ones.

 Another good indicator is whether your own parents enjoyed parenting.

492

Is your dating philosophy influenced mostly by men or women?

♥ Where do most of your ideas come from?

493

What was your significant other like as a young boy?

♥ Ask him. Men love to talk about themselves.

♥ Was he close to his mom?

Do you ever think about whether you really miss dating when you hit a dry spell, or is it a nice break for you?

If you like solitude, why not give up serious dating until you really want to be involved with someone?

495

Do you ever think about your significant other's grade point average?

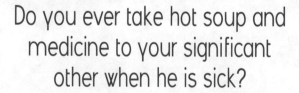 Most women want to marry someone they feel is intelligent.

496

Do you ever take hot soup and medicine to your significant other when he is sick?

Little things mean a lot. Everyone loves a thoughtful gesture.

How does your skin look and feel?

♥ Take good care of it.

♥ If you have problems with your complexion, make an appointment with a good dermatologist.

> If there were NONE who were discontented with what they have, the world would never reach for anything better.
>
> Florence Nightingale

498

What do you do to cheer yourself up after a bad date?

💜 Many women feel that talking it over with a friend or family member is the best medicine.

💜 Many women take themselves out on a shopping spree.

💜 Too many women blame themselves for a bad date!

> Don't take life too seriously.
> Elbert Hubbard

499

Do you ever send flowers to the man in your life?

♥ According to a national floral society, most men love receiving flowers.

500

Do you ever think about getting a makeover?

♥ Maybe you need an overhaul.

♥ What have you got to lose?

501

Do you ever think about going a bit more glamorous?

♥ Try a new style on your next date. How does it make you feel?

502

Do you ever think about getting some personal cards printed?

♥ They come in handy when men ask for your telephone number.

♥ For safety reasons, avoid putting your address on the cards.

503

Do you ever think about office romances?

♥ Know your company's policy regarding inter-office dating.

♥ Keep in mind that it can get tricky when you date your superior.

504

Do you ever date more than one man at a time?

♥ Many singles prefer to date only one person at a time.

♥ Dating more than one person can get very complicated.

505

How do you feel about yourself when you are in love?

♥ Most people are much kinder to themselves.

506

Do you ever think about getting a male pen pal?

♥ It is always nice to have friends of the opposite sex.

507

Would you be willing to move to a foreign country to help your husband's career path?

💜 Are there certain countries that you wouldn't be willing to move to?

💜 What would happen to your career if you moved?

> We must be willing to get rid of the life we've planned, so as to have the life that is waiting for us.
>
> Joseph Campbell

508

Do you ever think about hiring a professional photographer to take your picture?

Give a nice photo to all of your friends and family to carry so that they can show you off to any single guys they know.

509

Do you ever exaggerate your dating mistakes?

Take it easy on yourself.

Stop creating drama.

510

Do you make dating harder than it really needs to be?

💜 Many women spend so much time worrying about their love lives and that just brings on added stress.

💜 Give up the worry habit.

💜 Simplify. Simplify.

> It is better to be embarrassed than ashamed.
> The Talmud

511

What is your own definition of true intimacy?

💜 Do you believe in telling all to your mate, or are you more private with your thoughts and feelings?

💜 What do you expect from a mate regarding intimacy?

> If you do not tell the truth about yourself you cannot tell it about other people.
>
> Virginia Woolf

512

Do your friends ever flirt with your boyfriend?

If they do and it bothers you, talk to them about it.

513

Do you ever flirt with your friends' boyfriends?

Real friends never do anything that would hurt their friends' feelings.

514

Do you enjoy doubling with your friends on dates?

♥ Refrain from letting friends pressure you into going out with them if you don't really enjoy it.

515

What is your flirting style?

♥ Do you enjoy flirting, or is it a social skill that you lack?

♥ If you enjoy it, then you are probably good at it.

516

Do you ever think about upgrading your wardrobe at turning points in your life?

♥ Many women buy a new wardrobe:

    After graduation

    For a new job

    After a big promotion

    As they age

    Whenever the clothing styles change dramatically

517

How willing are you to go out on a blind date?

♥ Blind dates aren't for the timid, but they can be lots of fun.

♥ Blind dates are a good time to make it a double date.

> What do you plan
> to do with your own wild
> and precious life?
>
> Mary Oliver

Are you good at blind dating?

💜 Singles with a sense of adventure are usually good on blind dates.

💜 Singles who trust other people's judgment are more likely to go on a blind date.

💜 Women are more willing to try a blind date than men are.

> Love may be blind, but jealousy sees too much.
>
> Folk saying

519

Do you ever think about the fact that even when you are the one to end a relationship, your heart still needs time to heal?

Never rush back into the dating scene after a difficult breakup.

After rain comes fair weather.

James Howell

5²⁰

Do you ever think about the fact that no one is perfect?

💜 Stop expecting the men you meet to be perfect.

💜 Stop expecting yourself to be perfect.

5²¹

Do you ever think about how time is a good test to find out if it really is true love?

💜 You can't rush love.

💜 The old adage that time will tell is true.

5²²

How long do you like to have between the first date and the follow-up call?

💜 Most women like to hear from their date within two to four days.

5²³

At what age would you like become a mom for the first time?

💜 Most women become moms before their twenty-eighth birthday.

5²⁴

Do you ever think about how the average couple only has 1.2 children and that you are likely to have an only child?

Did you grow up imagining your children playing together?

Most new discoveries are suddenly seen things that were always there.
Susanne K. Langer

5²5

Do you ever think about using the ancient art of Feng Shui in your home and office to improve your love life?

♥ Many people believe in this ancient art.

5²6

How would you feel if you found out that your current beau had been married before?

♥ What are your feelings regarding divorce?

What are your feelings regarding men-only clubs?

♥ How would you feel if your significant other belonged to such a club?

> People are always blaming their circumstances for what they are. I don't believe in circumstances. The people who get on in this world are the people who get up and look for the circumstances they want, and, if they can't find them, make them.
>
> George Bernard Shaw

5²⁸

Are you in denial over any emotional issues regarding your love life?

♥ Listen to your heart.

♥ Ask your best friend for her opinion.

5²⁹

How well do you and your current love interest handle conflict?

♥ Being able to disagree in a healthy manner is key to a happy marriage.

Do you ever think about taking a class to improve your social skills?

♥ Check the yellow pages in your phone book under etiquette to look for classes in your area.

♥ Check with local modeling schools for classes in social graces.

Decisions determine destiny.
Frederick Speakman

531

How does the number of hours you work impact your love life?

💙 If you work more than forty-five hours per week, your social life will automatically be impacted by a lack of free time.

532

What do your grooming habits say about you when people first meet you?

💙 A woman who is well put together is ten times more likely to make a good first impression than a woman who isn't.

533

How does your work culture influence your love life?

♥ Do you frequent restaurants that your coworkers like?

♥ Do you chose concerts and movies based on your coworkers' opinions?

♥ Do you group date with coworkers?

♥ Do you attend company events with dates?

> Maybe being oneself is always an acquired taste.
> Patricia Hample

534

Do you ever think about the fact that, according to a recent poll, having a happy marriage is important to 98 percent of singles?

That is a comforting fact!

Let us not fear the hidden.

Muriel Rukeyser

535

Do you ever think about how stonewalling is one of the biggest relationship killers?

♥ Always keep the doors of communication open.

536

Do you ever think about how chronic workaholism can be a sign of a serious personality disorder?

♥ Never confuse a hardworking guy with a man who hides from life through his work.

537

Do you ever think about how love is supposed to be fun?

♥ Many singles report that looking for love is anything but fun.

538

Do you ever think about your dating secrets?

♥ What do you keep hidden and why?

♥ Maybe it is time to share some with a trusted friend.

539

How would you like being married to a public figure?

If you really value your privacy, this road probably isn't for you.

540

Do you ever listen to hear God's guidance regarding your love life?

Many people pray for direction and then fail to wait for an answer.

What would your life be like if you really did marry a prince?

♥ Countries all over the world still have royalty.

♥ However, the odds are not in your favor for marrying a real-life prince.

A good home is
better than riches.

Cervantes

542

Do you ever try to mother the man in your life?

♥ Stop that. He already has a mom. You need to be his girlfriend.

543

Do you ever think about the reasons why dating shows are so popular?

♥ People like to see how others handle their love lives.

544

Do you ever think about the topics you discuss on dates?

♥ Make sure that they are subjects that would be appealing to the opposite sex.

♥ Keep them upbeat.

> A good woman inspires a man,
> a brilliant woman interests him,
> a beautiful woman fascinates him—
> the sympathetic woman gets him.
>
> Helen Rowland

545

How do you handle it when other women flirt with your man?

❤ It could be seen as a good thing that others find your taste in men so attractive.

❤ Always remain calm and self-assured.

❤ If you lose him to another, then he wasn't right for you anyway, and therefore the other woman has done you a big favor.

546

Do you look men in the eyes when you talk to them?

♥ It shows self-confidence.

♥ Plus, it can be quite flirty.

547

Do you ever think about what subjects are off-limits on first or second dates?

♥ Many singles feel that they shouldn't discuss past loves in depth, politics, or skeletons in one's closet on early dates.

How much or how little do you share with your mother regarding your love life?

💜 Many women say that they share much of their love-life stories with their moms.

💜 Singles reveal that the hardest part of sharing with a parent is telling how they were mistreated by a boyfriend. If the couple gets back together, many parents have trouble forgiving the boyfriend even when the daughter has forgiven him.

Do you wear your heart on your sleeve?

The less sensitive you are to the little slights in life, the easier it will be to thrive in the dating world.

> If you can learn from hard knocks, you can also learn from soft touches.
>
> Carolyn Kenmore

550

Do you try to make old boyfriends jealous?

When a relationship is over, you will be happiest if you just forget your old flame and don't send any attention his way.

No company is preferable to bad company because we are more apt to catch the vices of others than their virtues, as disease is far more contagious than health.

C. C. Colton

551

Are you are a drama queen?

♥ Check with your friends.

♥ Ask your mom.

♥ Most men say that they relish a peaceful relationship.

> He who cannot change the very fabric of his thoughts will never be able to change reality.
>
> Anwar Sadat

552

Do you ever think about asking your significant other's friends about his old girlfriends, his lifestyle, or what he says about you?

♥ Proceed with caution here!

♥ If his friends mention your questions to him, it could cause a major problem for you with him. Plus, his friends might resent your prying.

553

What causes you to get butterflies in your stomach?

♥ First dates, first phone calls, and first kisses give many people a case of butterflies.

554

Would you be willing to marry a bad kisser if you really loved the man?

♥ Sex isn't everything, but it is a major component of marriage.

555

Do you ever think about answering or placing a classified ad?

💜 Many city magazines are filled with singles' ads.

💜 Newspapers are also full of the ads.

💜 Use caution here. You never know whom you might be dealing with.

> Too many people quit looking for love when they find a date.
>
> UNKNOWN

What you would think of your significant other if he were married to your sister or best friend instead of you?

Would he still seem so wonderful when you can look at him through the eyes of detachment?

Taking joy in life is a woman's best cosmetic.

Rosalind Russell

557

Do you dress to impress men or women?

♥ Try dressing to impress yourself. Then you will be more authentic.

558

Do you ever act too schoolgirlish around the opposite sex?

♥ Grow up!

♥ Act your age. Be who you are.

559

Do you ever make New Year's resolutions regarding your love life?

♥ Put into writing what you want out of life.

♥ Design a plan to make it happen.

♥ Share it with a friend for support.

> Where attention goes,
> energy flows.
> James Redfield

560

Do you have a friend that you can share everything with regarding your love life?

It can be a great comfort to have such a buddy.

It is cheaper than therapy.

The greatest good you can do for another is not just to share your riches, but to reveal to him his own.

Benjamin Disraeli

561

Do you ever think about taking a peek at your significant other's planner?

♥ Ask yourself what it is that you are looking for.

♥ Do you fear that he is being unfaithful?

♥ Do you worry that he doesn't have enough time for a relationship?

Do you ever think about decorating your house with fresh flowers when you have a date coming over for dinner?

💜 They can look pretty as a centerpiece.

💜 They add a touch of romance.

💜 Many flowers add wonderful fragrance to a room.

💜 It will let him know that you like flowers, hint hint.

Do you ever think about how your lifestyle, depending on your income, would be different if you married a poor man versus a rich man?

♥ Be sure that you are comfortable with the man (and his lifestyle) that you choose to marry.

Solitude is often the best society.

Ray Ray

564

Do you ever think about snooping when you are over at his place?

♥ You can tell a ton about someone from the way that they live and their possessions without snooping. Just be observant.

565

Do you ever think about double dating with a former boyfriend?

♥ Some singles remain friends with their exes without any problems.

566

If you have been dating
the same person for a long
time, do you ever think about
whether you really love him
or if your relationship is
just convenient?

Many singles find it hard to end a relationship
because they are scared to move on to the
unknown.

women's styles may
change, but their designs
remain the same.

Oscar Wilde

567

Do you ever think about how the qualities that you are searching so hard to find in a mate might not be important to you ten years from now?

Many women who are still in college are looking for a popular man who is extremely handsome and a good student. Many older women wouldn't give much weight to those qualifications.

Tastes change with time.

568

Do you dress like your peer group?

♥ If you dress too far out from the crowd, it will be harder to attract dates. This fact may not seem fair, but it is a sad reality of the dating world.

> And the day came when the risk to remain tight in the bud was more painful than the risk it took to blossom.
>
> Anaïs Nin

569

What would it be like if your mate had an ex-wife?

♥ Would you be OK having to deal with her?

♥ Would you be jealous?

♥ Would you constantly be comparing yourself to her?

Life has a way of evening things up: for every woman who makes a fool out of some man there's another who makes a man out of some fool.

UNKNOWN

570

Do you ever think about how you would feel doubling with your significant other's old flame?

Before you rule this out, just remember that she could be a source of great insight to you.

571

How would your dream date go?

What activities would take place?

Who would be your escort?

What would you wear?

572

How would you feel about being a stepmother?

💜 Stop buying into the mean fairytale version of the evil stepmom.

💜 If you are involved with a man who has children, give this tons of serious thought before you say, "I do."

The final word is love.
Dorothy Day

573

How do you act in front of his children?

♥ Be respectful about their mother.

♥ Refrain from trying to mother them.

♥ Develop a tough skin if they resent you at first.

♥ Plan fun family-style activities for the times you will all be together.

♥ Be sincere and natural. Kids hate fakes.

574

Are you good at making small talk?

♥ This skill will serve you well when you:

  Meet eligible men
  Meet friends of your significant other
  Meet his folks
  Meet his boss and coworkers

♥ Safe subjects for small talk are:

  Current events
  Pop culture
  Sports
  Big weather stories

575

Do you ever think about planting a flower garden so that you'll have a great supply of fresh flowers?

♥ Add a touch of homegrown romance by creating a wonderful garden.

576

At what point do you like to take a man home to meet your parents?

♥ Keep in mind that meeting a woman's parents can send serious-relationship signals to a man.

At what point in a relationship do you want to meet your boyfriend's parents?

♥ You can tell a great deal about a man from meeting his family.

♥ You can learn a lot by seeing where he grew up.

♥ You can learn a ton by watching the way he treats his mother.

578

At what point for you does a man change from being a date to being a boyfriend?

♥ Is the change based on the number of times you have gone out or on your feelings for the man?

♥ Many single women say that the change occurs once the relationship becomes exclusive.

> Be nice to people on your way up because you'll meet them on your way down.
>
> W.C. Fields

579

How many times have you been dumped?

♥ Take heart. The past doesn't have to repeat itself.

♥ Remember that it only takes one great guy to turn happily ever after into reality for you.

580

How many men have you dumped?

♥ Do you feel good about how you treat men once you decide to end a relationship?

Are you a manipulator?

💜 Let people behave in the ways that are natural to them.

💜 If you find yourself trying to manipulate your date's behavior, stop yourself and let go of your need to control.

💜 Ask yourself why you feel you need to manipulate others.

> There are only two ways to live your life. One is as though nothing is a miracle. The other is as though everything is a miracle.
>
> Albert Einstein

582

Do you ever think about your old hometown honey?

♥ If you do, try to set up a visit during your next trip home.

583

Do you ever think about how male drivers of red sports cars get more speeding tickets than any other group of drivers?

♥ What does that say about these men?

584

Do you ever think about what it would be like to be linked to a man in one of the following professions?

♥ Spy

♥ Soldier

♥ Peace Corps volunteer

♥ Gynecologist

♥ Fashion designer

♥ Actor

♥ Emergency-room physician

585

Do you ever think about trying a daring activity on your next date to get his heart pumping a bit faster?

💜 Consider:

A day hang gliding

A tandem parachute jump

Parasailing

💜 Research shows that when couples experience an emotionally charged event, they often transfer some of those exciting feelings to their companion.

586

Do you ever think about using your good stuff for everyday?

♥ Break out your fine china, silver, and crystal. Make every day seem special.

♥ Wear your good jewelry to the grocery store.

♥ Stop saving your best garments for a special occasion. Wear them before the styles change.

♥ Get it into your head that you deserve to be treated specially all of the time.

Do you ever think about the shopping style of your significant other?

💜 If you love shopping, just remember that most men don't.

💜 Many men only go to the mall when they actually need something.

💜 More men than women shop on the Internet.

💜 Many single men say that they don't enjoy going shopping with their girlfriends.

588

Do members of the opposite sex take you seriously?

💜 Blondes have a harder time being taken seriously than brunettes.

💜 Women with high-pitched voices are taken less seriously by both men and women.

> To be rooted is perhaps
> the most important and least
> recognized need of the human soul.
> Simon Weil

589

What would it take for you to approach a handsome stranger in a public place?

♥ Never waste an opportunity to meet a great guy. Create your own excuse for meeting him.

♥ Asking for directions is usually a good conversation starter in such a situation.

♥ You can always ask if the man has the time.

Don't wait. The time will never be just right.
Napoleon Hill

590

How does New Year's Eve make you feel?

♥ Do you like where your life is headed?

♥ Do you make resolutions? Do they include ones about your love life?

591

Do you believe the theory that men are from Mars and women are from Venus?

♥ Remember that we are all still human beings who want to be loved and appreciated.

592

Do you ever think about the boys you liked in grade school and junior high?

♥ What kind of boys were you drawn to back then?

♥ Has your taste changed?

♥ Have you learned anything about the opposite sex since those days?

> A little nonsense now and then is relished by the wisest men.
>
> Willy Wonka and the Chocolate Factory

593

Do you ever think about how boys and girls play differently?

♥ Even as babies there are differences between the sexes. Many women expect men to behave like their female friends, which can be the beginning of some major disappointments.

♥ Let men be men and enjoy the differences between the sexes.

594

Do you ever think about
how writing down your goals
increases the chance that
you will reach them?

If you want something wonderful to happen in
your love life, turn it into a goal and write it
down. Place the goals where you will see them
every day.

Raise your sail one
foot and you get ten
feet of wind.

Chinese proverb

595

Do you ever think about dating one of your boyfriend's friends?

♥ Many couples have met through dating a friend of their old love interest. However, this can be a very tricky situation, so if you decide to proceed here, do so with extreme caution.

> If you're not failing now and again, it's a sign you're playing it safe.
>
> Woody Allen

596

After a breakup, do you often focus on just the good times without remembering the bad?

♥ Keep your perspective.

♥ Focus on the whole picture.

♥ The average person has sixty thousand thoughts per day.

The eyes of my eyes are opened.
E.E. Cummings

597

Do you ever think about spending more of your free time just hanging out in places that men frequent?

💜 Grab some friends and promise yourselves that you all will meet some great guys while you enjoy each other's company.

The most exhausting thing you can do is to be inauthentic.
ANNe Morrow Lindbergh

598

Do you ever think about ordering a subscription to a bridal magazine even though you are presently unattached?

♥ Whoever said that those magazines were just for brides to be?

♥ Indulge your fantasy.

The gift of fantasy has meant more to me than my talent for absorbing positive knowledge.

Albert Einstein

599

Are you too trusting or gullible?

♥ Ask your friends for their opinions.

♥ Do men ever take advantage of your good nature?

600

How would you feel if you had a higher income than your spouse?

♥ Would you feel proud of yourself or disappointed in your mate?

What would you do if your boyfriend wanted to date around and you wanted the relationship to be exclusive?

 Would you draw the line?

 Would you continue to see him?

 Would you begin to date others?

 Would you break it off?

602

Would you want your mate with you during childbirth?

♥ The majority of couples now share in the child-birth experience.

603

Would you marry or even date a man who has spent time behind bars?

♥ What proof would you need that he had reformed?

Would you want to marry a man who hasn't earned the level of education that you have earned?

💜 More and more women are graduating from college and post-graduate programs.

💜 The number of women marrying men with less education than they have is on the rise.

> Decision is a risk rooted in the courage of being free.
>
> Paul Tillich

605

Do you ever think about how much time you spend getting ready for a date?

💜 Is he worth it?

606

Do you ever think about your figure?

💜 The obesity rate for the United States is twenty percent.

💜 Men consistently rank a woman's figure as an important factor in attraction.

607

How often do you look at yourself in a mirror?

♥ Are you happy with what you see?

608

How much like your mom are you in your views regarding the opposite sex?

♥ If you are very alike, is she happy and well adjusted?

♥ Remember always to follow your own heart.

609

Are you a simple or complex kind of woman?

♥ There is no right or wrong answer here, for we are all individuals.

610

How long do you think you would last in a long-distance romance?

♥ What would bother you the most? Why?

How old would a man have to be before you would choose not to date him even if he were wonderful?

💜 Huge differences in age can be a big obstacle for couples to overcome in long-term relationships.

To thine own self be true.

William Shakespeare

612

How much younger would a man have to be before you would choose not to date him even though you were highly attracted to him?

♥ Would it bother you to have people saying that you were robbing the cradle? Why? Men have been doing it for years.

Love is what happens to a man and a woman who don't know each other.

W. Somerset Maugham

613

Would your love life be
dramatically different
if you were one of the
following stereotypes?

💜 Southern belle

💜 Surfer girl

💜 Female jock

💜 Socialite

💜 Model

💜 Soldier

What kind of mother will you be one day?

♥ Do you want to be a full-time mom or a working mother?

> Backward, turn backward
> O time in flight;
> Make me a child again
> Just for tonight.
>
> Elizabeth Allen

Would you be willing to move to another city just to be near a boyfriend, or would he have to be a fiancé for you to even consider the move?

💜 Follow your head and your heart.

💜 Do what is in your best interest.

💜 Many women have moved to be near a boyfriend only to have the relationship end and find themselves stuck in a city where they don't want to live.

616

Do you ever send the man
in your life a card when
you can't seem to express
yourself verbally?

♥ You can find cards for all situations at your local
card shop.

♥ Everyone likes to get a little surprise mail from
their sweetie.

> A prudent man profits from
> personal experience, a wise one
> from the experience of others.
>
> Dr. Joseph Collins

617

Do you ever think about how women are generally more comfortable sharing their feelings than men?

♥ From childhood, girls are more expressive regarding their feelings than boys.

♥ Research proves that little girls will talk longer about subjects than boys.

> What passes for woman's intuition is often nothing more than man's transparency.
>
> George Jean Nathan

618

Do you ever dream about petting a cat?

♥ Many dream experts believe that this is a common theme in dreams that signifies that a person is searching for love.

619

Do you take full advantage of technology in your love life?

♥ Carry a cell phone to stay connected.

♥ Email your boyfriend when you can't get together.

Did you know that the average length of a marriage for couples that divorce is just over seven years?

The notion of the seven-year itch is based in reality.

It is the soul's duty to be loyal to its own desires. It must abandon itself to its own master passion.

Rebecca West

621

Do you ever think about how working women are more interested in flexible hours and childcare than their male coworkers?

It is still the wife's job in the majority of marriages to take the primary role of caretaker for the couple's children.

Do you ever think about how long it might take you to get pregnant if you are over thirty?

 The number of couples who are undergoing fertility treatments is on the rise.

Would you be willing to marry a man who cannot have children?

 Search your soul for what is right for you.

Do you ever think about doing something a bit outrageous to express your feelings for the man in your life?

❤ Try:

Renting a billboard to say you care

Placing an ad in the classifieds

Hiring a skywriter

Sending a singing telegram

Placing a giant sign in his yard

Sending a ton of greeting cards instead of just one

Throwing a big surprise party to celebrate your relationship

625

How would you handle being married to a night owl if you are a morning person or vice versa?

♥ The average person requires between six and eight hours of sleep per night. When you get those hours is not important to your health, but it can be very important to your lifestyle.

> Be faithful to that which exists nowhere but in yourself—and thus make yourself indispensable.
>
> Andre Gide

626

How would you deal with it if your mate had to work third shift?

♥ Would you be willing to change your routine around to accommodate time together?

627

Do you ever think about how love can heal a broken heart?

♥ Be careful not to jump into a new relationship too quickly, but "out with the old and in with the new" does heal many a broken heart.

628

What lessons can you learn from other women's love lives?

♥ Look and learn. Take note of what makes others successful at the dating game.

629

Whom do you call in times of great joy or great sadness?

♥ Is your significant other one of the first?

630

Do you ever think about calling a childhood friend to renew your friendship?

💜 Who knows, she might have a great single brother, friend, or coworker who would be just perfect for you!

631

What would you do if all of the men on the planet disappeared for a year?

💜 Would you be relieved or heartbroken?

632

Do you ever think about creating an advisory board to help you with your love life?

♥ Consider a team that includes each of the following:

A fashion advisor

A happily married woman

A male friend

A socially active gal pal

Tell everyone what you want to do and someone will want to help you do it.

W. Clement Stone

633

Do you ever think about
how many singles are
totally unprepared for the
reality of marriage?

💜 Before you say, "I do," get some premarital
counseling with your significant other.

💜 Have many in-depth conversations with your
married friends .

> It is better to have
> loved and lost than to
> never have loved at all.
>
> Samuel Butler

634

Do you ever think about asking your youngest sibling or your friend's child for their opinion regarding your current love interest?

♥ Kids are so honest that you might learn something important this way.

♥ Children are naturally intuitive and they might pick up on something that you in your sophistication have overlooked.

635

Do you ever think about using milestone birthdays as stepping stones to a better love life?

❤ Instead of dreading the big 30 or 40, why not use it as an inspiration to make the next thirty years even better?

> What would happen if one woman told the truth about her life? The world would split open.
>
> Muriel Rukeyser

636

Do you ever think about getting subscriptions to magazines that are targeted for male readers?

♥ They might provide you with some great subjects to discuss over your next date.

♥ They might give you a new insight into the male mind.

♥ You might find a new interest or hobby among the pages.

637

Do you ever think about using the seasons to broaden your social circle?

💙 Get outside more in warm weather and mingle.

💙 During the winter months join a new club, entertain, or participate in winter sports.

💙 Take advantage of long summer nights to get to know your neighbors.

💙 Attend any holiday events where singles might go.

638

Do you ever think about how if you meet one single man each week, that by the end of the year you will have fifty-two new contacts?

♥ Networking is a key to successful dating.

> Connections are made slowly, sometimes they grow underground.
>
> Marge Piercy

639

Do you ever think about how most men become less romantic after marriage?

♥ If your current love interest isn't romantic now, don't expect him to be Don Juan after the wedding.

640

Do you ever think about marrying a rich man?

♥ According to Dinesh D'Souza, author of The Moral Conundrum of Success, you have to have a net worth of ten to one hundred million dollars to be considered rich in the United States. To be considered super-rich, you need personal wealth of more than one hundred million dollars.

How do your political views influence your love life?

 Do you only feel comfortable with men who share your views?

 Would you date a man who belonged to a different political party?

 Try working for your favorite candidate during the next election as it is a great way to meet single men.

> Many men go fishing all of their lives without knowing that it is not fish they are after.
>
> Henry David Thoreau

642

What do you daydream about and what does it mean?

♥ Where do you go in your private world?

♥ What brings you joy?

643

Do you ever think about not hiding the truth from yourself any longer?

♥ Denial is never helpful.

516

Do you ever think about getting a new career where you might meet more men?

💜 Teachers and librarians report the lowest levels of job satisfaction when it comes to meeting exciting men.

💜 Be creative so that you can meet more men and still love your work.

> You can live a lifetime and, at the end of it, know more about other people than you know about yourself.
>
> beryl Markham

645

Have you ever dated certain men just to please your family or friends?

♥ Look out for this trap.

♥ In love and life, you must be true to yourself.

646

Do you ever think about all of the things you have learned in school and yet how little you know about yourself?

♥ Look inside. Go within.

647

Does it seem like it is
taking forever for Mr. Right
to come into your life?

♥ Relax, he will come along and when he does you
will no longer care about how long it took.

648

Do you ever think about
how lonely a bad
marriage would feel?

♥ Never jump into marriage.

♥ Solitude is preferable to an unhappy marriage.

649

If you had just arrived on this planet today, what you would think about:

💜 Dating

💜 Romance

💜 Love

💜 Marriage

💜 Men

> Life is short and it's up to you to make it sweet.
>
> Sadie Delaney

650

Do you ever think about why this book made its way into your hands and what you are supposed to gain from reading it?

💙 What questions resonated with you?

💙 What insights have you gained?

💙 What changes do you intend to make?

About the Author

Cyndi Haynes is the author of eleven best-selling books, including *2002 Things to Do on a Date*, *2002 Romantic Ideas*, and *2002 Ways to Show Your Kids You Love Them*. Her books have been published in fifteen languages and have been written about in numerous publications including *Cosmopolitan*, *Redbook*, and *Marie Claire*. She has appeared on hundreds of radio and television programs. She lives in Indiana with her husband, son, and three dogs.